DDS

KEYWORD
REFERENCE

James Coolbaugh

A Division of
DUKE COMMUNICATIONS INTERNATIONAL

221 E. 29th Street • Loveland, CO 80538
(800) 621-1544 • (970) 663-4700 • www.29thStreetPress.com

Library of Congress Cataloging-in-Publication Data

Coolbaugh, James, 1961-
   DDS keyword reference / by James Coolbaugh.
   p. cm.
   Includes index.
   ISBN 1-58304-042-0 (pbk.)
   1. Data structures (Computer science) 2. File organization
(Computer science) 3. IBM AS/400 (Computer)--Programming. I. Title.
   QA76.9.D35 C67 1999
   005.7'3--dc21
                                                99-6158
                                                CIP

Published by 29th Street Press
DUKE COMMUNICATIONS INTERNATIONAL
Loveland, Colorado

Copyright © 1999 by James Coolbaugh

This book was printed and bound in Canada.

ISBN 1-58304-042-0

2001 2000 1999 WL 10 9 8 7 6 5 4 3 2 1

This book is dedicated to my wife

Pam

and my children

Michael and Hannah,

whose loving support,

encouragement,

and patience

made this publication possible.

Table of Contents

Chapter 5 Intersystem Communications Function (ICF) Files

Introduction

With the introduction of the System/38 in the early 1980s, IBM provided a mechanism for creating files from external source specifications called Data Description Specifications (DDS). From DDS source, you can create file objects (object type *FILE on the AS/400) that high-level language (HLL) programs can then use. This approach eliminates the need to hard-code file specifications in every HLL program that uses a specific file. Creating files from DDS source is called *external file definition.*

THE A-SPECIFICATION FORMAT

You can use DDS to create physical, logical, display, printer, and ICF files. All file types are coded using a format called the A-specification (A-spec). The A-spec is a combination of fixed-format and free-format definitions used to specify a particular file.

The A-spec consists of three areas: the conditioning zone, the definition zone, and the keyword zone.

Conditioning Zone

The conditioning zone of the A-spec encompasses column 7 through column 16. Within the conditioning zone for display, printer, and ICF files, you can use indicators to control when fields or keywords are active for the file (indicators are not valid for physical and logical file specifications). You can place up to three conditioning indicators (e.g., 99 or N99) and a single letter code (A for "and" or O for "or") in an A-spec to combine the conditions of two or more consecutive specifications into a single, complex condition.

Definition Zone

The definition zone spans columns 17 through 44 of the A-spec. This zone is coded strictly in fixed format, in which the meaning of the letters, digits, and symbols depends on the column in which you place them. The definition zone, as its name implies, lets you define data fields (input, output, or both) and record formats.

Keyword Zone

From column 45 through column 80 of the A-spec, you can plug in any number of *keywords* in free-format style. Like command parameters, keywords for the most part consist of an uppercase name (of up to 10 characters) followed by a value enclosed in parentheses.

THIS BOOK'S FOCUS

This book focuses on the keyword zone. Literally hundreds of keywords exist, and the ones you can use in a particular situation depends on the type of file you're creating: physical, logical, display, printer, or ICF. Separate sections of this book cover all the keywords for each of the five file types. Each section discusses all keywords for that file type in alphabetical order. Each keyword discussion lists all the keyword's parameters, explains the use of the keyword, and shows an example of how to code the keyword and parameters in the A-specs.

Chapter 1

Physical Files

Physical files are used to store actual data. To create a physical file, you specify how the data in the file is defined.

Every physical file has one and only one record format. You can optionally specify that an index be created in connection with the physical file.

DATA TYPES

There are nine valid data types for physical files, as listed in the following table.

Code	Meaning
P	Packed decimal
S	Zoned decimal
B	Binary
F	Floating point
A	Character
H	Hexadecimal
L	Date
T	Time
Z	Timestamp

You code each field's data type in column 35. If you leave column 35 blank, the field defaults to type A for character fields and P for numeric fields.

FIELD USAGE

Every field defined in a physical file is available for both input and output. Therefore, you can leave the usage column (column 38) blank or use a value of B (meaning both input and output are allowed). No other values are valid for physical files.

KEYWORD LEVELS

For physical files, you can specify keywords at four distinct levels: file level, record-format level, field level, and key level.

Keywords coded at the file level affect the entire physical file. These keywords are placed before the record format in the DDS source.

Record format-level keywords affect the physical file's record format and consequently, because a physical file has only one record format, the format of the entire file. You define a record format by coding an R in column 17 of the A-spec, before the first field defined in the record format.

Field-level keywords affect an individual field in the record format.

Key-level keywords are specified on fields defined as part of the key (index) for the physical file. You define a key by coding a K in column 17 of the A-spec. Key definitions must be placed after the last field defined for the record format in the DDS source.

KEYWORDS

ABSVAL (Absolute Value)

Level	Parameters
Key	None

This keyword tells the AS/400 to ignore the sign of a numeric field when creating an index for the physical file — in other words, to treat negative numbers as positive numbers for index purposes. The database value remains negative.

```
....1....+....2....+....3....+....4....+....5....+....6....+....7....+....8
A           R SLSFMT
A             CUSNBR        7P 0
A             CUSNAM        35A
A             ORDNBR        7P 0
A             SLSAMT        9P 2
A           K SLSAMT                      ABSVAL
```

ALIAS (Alternative Name)

Level	Parameters
Field	1) Alternate name

This keyword lets you assign a name longer than 10 characters for a field. If your HLL program supports longer field names, this alias definition is used; otherwise, it is ignored.

PARAMETER DEFINITION

Alternate name

The alternate name can be up to 30 characters long.

```
....1....+....2....+....3....+....4....+....5....+....6....+....7....+....8
A           R CUSFMT
A             CUSNBR        7P 0       ALIAS(CUSTOMER_NUMBER)
A             CUSNAM        35A        ALIAS(CUSTOMER_NAME)
```

ALTSEQ (Alternate Collating Sequence)

Level	Parameters
File	1) Table name

The ALTSEQ keyword tells the AS/400 to use an alternate sequencing table when creating the index for the physical file.

PARAMETER DEFINITION

Table name

This parameter is the name of the alternate collating-sequence table to be used. You can optionally qualify the table name with the name of the library, as in the second example below.

```
....1....+....2....+....3....+....4....+....5....+....6....+....7....+....8
A                                       ALTSEQ(UPPERCASE)
A          R CUSFMT
A            CUSNBR        7P 0
A            CUSNAM       35A
A          K CUSNAM

....1....+....2....+....3....+....4....+....5....+....6....+....7....+....8
A                                       ALTSEQ(PRODLIB/UPPERCASE)
A          R CUSFMT
A            CUSNBR        7P 0
A            CUSNAM       35A
A          K CUSNAM
```

ALWNULL (Allow Null Value)

Level	Parameters
Field	None

This keyword tells the AS/400 that null values are allowed in the field when records are written to the physical file. Null values are not the same as blanks or zeros.

```
....1....+....2....+....3....+....4....+....5....+....6....+....7....+....8
A          R CUSFMT
A            CUSNBR        7P 0
A            CUSNAM       35A
A            CUSAD1       35A         ALWNULL
```

CCSID (Coded Character Set Identifier)

Level	Parameters
File	1) Value
Field	2) Display length (optional)

This keyword lets you specify the number of the coded character set to be used for character fields in the physical file. When you specify CCSID at the file level, all character fields are affected. Otherwise, only those fields containing CCSID are affected.

PARAMETER DEFINITIONS

Value

This parameter is a number up to five digits long that corresponds to a specific coded character set. For a list of valid codes, see IBM's *National Language Support* manual.

Field Display Length

This optional parameter lets you define the displayable length of the field on the screen when the field is referenced on a display.

```
....1....+....2....+....3....+....4....+....5....+....6....+....7....+....8
A                                          CCSID(37)
A         R CUSFMT
A           CUSNBR       7P 0
A           CUSNAM       35A
A           CUSAD1       35A

....1....+....2....+....3....+....4....+....5....+....6....+....7....+....8
A           CCSID(37)
A         R CUSFMT
A           CUSNBR       7P 0
A           CUSNAM       35A       CCSID(500 30)
A           CUSAD1       35A
```

CHECK (Check)

Level	Parameters
Field	1) Edit check code

This keyword does not affect the physical file itself. When a display file references a physical file field on which you've coded the CHECK keyword, CHECK provides default validity checking. See the discussion of the CHECK keyword in Chapter 3 for more information about how CHECK affects the screen field.

PARAMETER DEFINITION

Edit check code

This parameter is a character code that must be one of the following values:

Code	Meaning
AB	Allow blank
ME	Mandatory enter
MF	Mandatory fill
M10	Modulus 10 self-check
M10F	Modulus 10 self-check
M11	Modulus 11 self-check
M11F	Modulus 11 self-check
VN	Validate name
VNE	Validate name extended

You can specify more than one code in the CHECK keyword.

```
....1....+....2....+....3....+....4....+....5....+....6....+....7....+....8
A           R CUSFMT
A             CUSNBR        7P 0      CHECK(M10 MF)
A             CUSNAM       35A        CHECK(ME)
A             CUSAD1       35A
```

CHKMSGID (Check Message Identifier)

Level	Parameters
FIELD	1) Message ID
	2) Message file
	3) Message data field (optional)

This keyword lets you specify a particular message ID to be used with the validity-checking keyword specified on the field. The specified message ID is used instead of the AS/400's default message.

When you reference this field in a display file, the CHKMSGID keyword is copied to the display file. You can specify CHKMSGID only when you use one of the following keywords: VALUES, RANGE, CMP, COMP, CHECK(M10), CHECK(M11), CHECK(VN), or CHECK(VNE).

PARAMETER DEFINITIONS

Message ID
This parameter is a seven-character identifier for the message to be used.

Message file
This parameter is the name of the file in which the message ID is located. You can qualify the file name with the library if you wish, as in the second example below.

Message data field

This optional parameter specifies the name of a field that contains data the message ID uses to format the message text properly. See the CHKMSGID keyword in Chapter 3 for more information about how this parameter works.

```
....1....+....2....+....3....+....4....+....5....+....6....+....7....+....8
A          R CUSFMT
A            CUSNBR      7P 0
A            CUSNAM     35A
A            RATING      1S 0        RANGE(1 5)
A                                    CHKMSGID(USR0001 USERMSGF)

....1....+....2....+....3....+....4....+....5....+....6....+....7....+....8
A          R CUSFMT
A            CUSNBR      7P 0
A            CUSNAM     35A
A            RATING      1S 0        RANGE(1 5)
A                                    CHKMSGID(USR0001 PRODLIB/USERMSGF +
A                                    &DATA)
```

CMP (Comparison)

Level	Parameters
Field	1) Relational operator
	2) Value

This keyword is the same as the COMP keyword. You should use the COMP keyword instead, however; CMP exists simply for backward compatibility.

COLHDG (Column Heading)

Level	Parameters
Field	1) Line 1
	2) Line 2 (optional)
	3) Line 3 (optional)

This keyword lets you specify up to three lines of text to be used as a column heading for the field. Many IBM utilities that allow data manipulation or listing in a physical file (e.g., Query/400, DFU) select these headings.

PARAMETER DEFINITIONS

Line 1

This parameter specifies up to 20 characters of text contained within apostrophes (').

Line 2

This parameter specifies up to 20 characters of text contained within apostrophes (').

Line 3

This parameter specifies up to 20 characters of text contained within apostrophes (').

```
....1....+....2....+....3....+....4....+....5....+....6....+....7....+....8
A          R SLSFMT
A            CUSNBR        7P 0     COLHDG('Customer' 'Number')
A            CUSNAM       35A       COLHDG('Customer' 'Name')
A            ORDNBR        7P 0     COLHDG('Order' 'Number')
A            SLSAMT        9P 2     COLHDG('Total' 'Sales' 'Amount')
```

COMP (Comparison)

Level	Parameters
Field	1) Relational operator
	2) Value

This keyword does not affect the physical file itself. When a display file references this physical file field, the COMP keyword is copied to provide default validity checking. Refer to the COMP keyword in Chapter 3 for more information about how this keyword affects the screen field.

PARAMETER DEFINITIONS

Relational operator

This parameter is a two-character code that specifies the type of comparison test to be performed.

Operator	Meaning
EQ	Equal to
NE	Not equal to
LT	Less than
NL	Not less than
GT	Greater than
NG	Not greater than
LE	Less than or equal to
GE	Greater than or equal to

Value

This parameter represents the specific value to be tested against. The value entered must be in the same format as the field definition.

```
....1....+....2....+....3....+....4....+....5....+....6....+....7....+....8
A          R SLSFMT
A            CUSNBR        7P 0
A            CUSNAM        35A          COMP(NE ' ')
A            ORDNBR        7P 0         COMP(GT 0)
A            SLSAMT        9P 2         COMP(GE 0)
```

DATFMT (Date Format)

Level	Parameters
Field	1) Date format

This keyword specifies the format of a date field (data type L). The length of the date field depends on the date-format parameter.

PARAMETER DEFINITION

Date format
This parameter is a code that represents the format of a date field. The table below shows all the valid values.

Code	Meaning	Format	Length
*JOB	Job default	Depends on job	—
*MDY	Month/day/year	mm/dd/yy	8
*DMY	Day/month/year	dd/mm/yy	8
*YMD	Year/month/day	yy/mm/dd	8
*JUL	Julian	yy/ddd	6
*ISO	International Standards Organization	yyyy-mm-dd	10
*USA	USA Standard	mm/dd/yyyy	10
*EUR	European Standard	dd.mm.yyyy	10
*JIS	Japanese Standard	yyyy-mm-dd	10

The default value for this parameter is *ISO.

```
....1....+....2....+....3....+....4....+....5....+....6....+....7....+....8
A          R CUSFMT
A            CUSNBR        7P 0
A            CUSNAM        35A
A            ENTDTE         L           DATFMT(*ISO)
```

DATSEP (Date Separator)

Level	Parameters
Field	1) Date separator

This keyword defines the separator to be used for a date field (data type L). If the date field is defined as *ISO, *USA, *EUR, or *JIS, you cannot specify this keyword.

PARAMETER DEFINITION

Date separator
This parameter is either an explicit value defined within apostrophes (') or a value of *JOB. The valid values are slash (/), dash (-), period (.), comma (,), and blank ( ). Special value *JOB indicates that the job's default separator is to be used.

```
....1....+....2....+....3....+....4....+....5....+....6....+....7....+....8
A              R CUSFMT
A                CUSNBR        7P 0
A                CUSNAM        35A
A                ENTDTE         L          DATFMT(*YMD)
A                                          DATSEP('.')
```

DESCEND (Descending Sequence)

Level	Parameters
Key	None

This keyword tells the AS/400 to sort the field in descending sequence when creating the index for the physical file.

```
....1....+....2....+....3....+....4....+....5....+....6....+....7....+....8
A              R SLSFMT
A                CUSNBR        7P 0
A                CUSNAM        35A
A                ORDNBR        7P 0
A                SLSAMT        9P 2
A              K SLSAMT                    DESCEND
```

DFT (Default)

Level	Parameters
Field	1) Default value

This keyword assigns a default value to a field.

PARAMETER DEFINITION

Default value
This parameter specifies a value to be the default for the field. The value entered must match the data type for the field (e.g., numeric value for numeric fields, character data for character fields). You can also specify a value of *NULL if you've coded the ALWNULL keyword on the field.

```
....1....+....2....+....3....+....4....+....5....+....6....+....7....+....8
A          R CUSFMT
A            CUSNBR        7P 0
A            CUSNAM       35A
A            CUSTYP        1A           DFT('A')
```

DIGIT (Digit)

Level	Parameters
Key	None

This keyword tells the AS/400 to use only the digit portion (the rightmost four bits) of each byte in a field to create the index for the physical file. The zone portion is set to zero. This keyword is valid for character, hexadecimal, and zoned-decimal fields (data types A, H, and S).

```
....1....+....2....+....3....+....4....+....5....+....6....+....7....+....8
A          R SLSFMT
A            CUSNBR        7P 0
A            CUSNAM       35A
A            ORDNBR        7P 0
A            SLSAMT        9P 2
A          K CUSNAM                     DIGIT
```

EDTCDE (Edit Code)

Level	Parameters
Field	1) Edit code
	2) Floating character (optional)

This keyword does not affect the physical file itself. When a display file references a field on which you've coded the EDTCDE keyword, the keyword provides default screen editing of the field. Refer to the EDTCDE keyword in Chapter 3 for a full discussion of the valid edit codes and how they look on the screen.

PARAMETER DEFINITIONS

Edit code

This parameter is a valid AS/400 edit code.

Floating character

This optional parameter is either an asterisk (*) or any other character designated to function as a floating currency symbol. An asterisk indicates that the numeric field is to have all leading zeros replaced with asterisks. The floating character appears to the left of the most significant digit.

```
....1....+....2....+....3....+....4....+....5....+....6....+....7....+....8
A          R SLSFMT
A            CUSNBR       7P 0       EDTCDE(4)
A            CUSNAM       35A
A            ORDNBR       7P 0       EDTCDE(4)
A            SLSAMT       9P 2       EDTCDE(L)
```

EDTWRD (Edit Word)

Level	Parameters
Key	1) Edit word

This keyword does not affect the physical file itself. When a display file references a field on which you've coded the EDTWRD keyword, the specified keyword provides default screen editing of the field. Refer to the discussion of the EDTWRD keyword in Chapter 3 for the complete explanation of how to define an edit word.

PARAMETER DEFINITION

Edit word
This parameter is a valid AS/400 edit-word character string.

```
....1....+....2....+....3....+....4....+....5....+....6....+....7....+....8
A          R PRSFMT
A            EMP#         7P 0
A            EMPNAM       35A
A            SSN          9P 0       EDTWRD('   - -   ')
```

FCFO (First-Changed First-Out)

Level	Parameters
File	None

This keyword tells the AS/400 that when duplicate records exist in the index for the physical file, the record that was changed first is to be retrieved first.

You cannot specify this keyword with the keywords FIFO, LIFO, or UNIQUE.

```
....1....+....2....+....3....+....4....+....5....+....6....+....7....+....8
A                                    FCFO
A          R SLSFMT
A            CUSNBR       7P 0
A            CUSNAM       35A
A            ORDNBR       7P 0
A            SLSAMT       9P 2
A          K SLSAMT
```

FIFO (First-In First-Out)

Level	Parameters
File	None

This keyword tells the AS/400 that when duplicate records exist in the index for the physical file, the record that was put into the file first is to be retrieved first.

You cannot specify this keyword with the keywords FCFO, LIFO, or UNIQUE.

```
....1....+....2....+....3....+....4....+....5....+....6....+....7....+....8
A                                           FIFO
A          R SLSFMT
A            CUSNBR        7P 0
A            CUSNAM       35A
A            ORDNBR        7P 0
A            SLSAMT        9P 2
A          K SLSAMT
```

FLTPCN (Floating-Point Precision)

Level	Parameters
Field	1) Precision

This keyword defines the precision of a floating-point field (data type F).

PARAMETER DEFINITION

Precision

This parameter has a value of either *SINGLE or *DOUBLE. Single-precision fields can contain up to 9 digits, whereas double-precision fields can contain up to 17 digits. The default is single precision.

```
....1....+....2....+....3....+....4....+....5....+....6....+....7....+....8
A          R SCIENCE
A            CALC1        17F 6      FLTPCN(*DOUBLE)
A            CALC2         8F 3      FLTPCN(*SINGLE)
A            CALC3         5F 2
```

FORMAT (Format)

Level	Parameters
Record	1) File name

This keyword references another database file on the AS/400 from which all the fields are to be shared. The record format name must exist in the other database file.

PARAMETER DEFINITION

File name

This parameter is the name of the database file in which the format name is to be found. You can qualify the file name with the name of the library if you wish, as in the second example below.

```
....1....+....2....+....3....+....4....+....5....+....6....+....7....+....8
A          R SLSFMT                    FORMAT(SALESHST)
....1....+....2....+....3....+....4....+....5....+....6....+....7....+....8
A          R SLSFMT                    FORMAT(PRODLIB/SALESHST)
```

LIFO (Last-In First-Out)

Level	Parameters
File	None

This keyword tells the AS/400 that when duplicate records exist in the index for the physical file, the record that was put into the file last is to be retrieved first. You cannot specify this keyword with the keywords FCFO, FIFO, or UNIQUE.

```
....1....+....2....+....3....+....4....+....5....+....6....+....7....+....8
A                                            LIFO
A          R SLSFMT
A            CUSNBR        7P 0
A            CUSNAM       35A
A            ORDNBR        7P 0
A            SLSAMT        9P 2
A          K SLSAMT
```

NOALTSEQ (No Alternate Collating Sequence)

Level	Parameters
Key	None

This keyword lets you override the effect of the ALTSEQ keyword specified at the file level. When you specify this keyword, the key field is not sequenced by the table specified in the ALTSEQ keyword.

```
....1....+....2....+....3....+....4....+....5....+....6....+....7....+....8
A                                            ALTSEQ(UPPERCASE)
A          R CUSFMT
A            CUSNBR        7P 0
A            CUSNAM       35A
A            CUSAD1       35A
A            CUSCTY       20A
A            CUSSTA        2A
A          K CUSSTA                     NOALTSEQ
A          K CUSCTY                     NOALTSEQ
A          K CUSNAM
```

RANGE (Range)

Level	Parameters
Field	1) Low value
	2) High value

This keyword does not affect the physical file itself. When a display file references the physical file field, the RANGE keyword provides default validity checking. For more information about how this keyword affects the screen field, see the RANGE keyword in Chapter 3.

PARAMETER DEFINITIONS

Low value

This parameter is the lower end of the valid range for the field. The value entered must be of the same type as the field definition (e.g., a number for numeric fields, a character for character fields).

High value

This parameter is the upper end of the valid range for the field. The value entered must be of the same type as the field definition.

The low and high values are included in the valid values for the field.

```
....1....+....2....+....3....+....4....+....5....+....6....+....7....+....8
A              R CUSFMT
A                CUSNBR        7P 0
A                CUSNAM       35A
A                CUSTER        3P 0        RANGE(1 150)
```

REF (Reference)

Level	Parameters
File	1) File name
	2) Record format name (optional)

This keyword specifies the name of the database file from which all field references are to be retrieved. A field is referenced when you code an R in column 29.

PARAMETER DEFINITIONS

File name

This parameter is the name of the database file from which references can be retrieved. You can qualify the file name with the library name if you wish, as in the second example below.

Record format name

This optional parameter specifies the particular record format in the database
file to use for field references.

```
....1....+....2....+....3....+....4....+....5....+....6....+....7....+....8
A                                        REF(REFFILE)
A          R SLSFMT
A            CUSNBR      R
A            CUSNAM      R
A            CUSAD1          35A
```

```
....1....+....2....+....3....+....4....+....5....+....6....+....7....+....8
A                                        REF(PRODLIB/REFFILE FORMAT1)
A          R SLSFMT
A            CUSNBR      R
A            CUSNAM      R
A            CUSAD1          35A
```

REFFLD (Referenced Field)

Level	Parameters
Field	1) Field name
	2) File name (optional)

This keyword lets you retrieve the field reference from a field in a file other
than that specified in the REF keyword.

PARAMETER DEFINITIONS

Field name

This parameter is the name of the field to reference in the other file. If the
specified file has more than one record format, you can optionally specify
the name of the record format in which the field is found.

File name

This parameter is the name of the file from which the field reference is to be
retrieved. You can specify either the file name or a value of *SRC. *SRC indicates
that the field reference exists within this same DDS source. If you don't specify a
file name, *SRC is the default. You can qualify the file name with the name of
the library if you wish.

```
....1....+....2....+....3....+....4....+....5....+....6....+....7....+....8
A                                        REF(REFFILE)
A          R RECORD1
A            PART#       R
A            ITEM            10A
A            ITEM1       R            REFFLD(ITEM)
A            ITEM2       R            REFFLD(RECORD1/ITEM)
A            ITEM3       R            REFFLD(ITEM *SRC)
A            ITEM4       R            REFFLD(ITEM FILE2)
A            ITEM5       R            REFFLD(ITEM PRODLIB/FILE2)
```

REFSHIFT (Reference Shift)

Level	Parameters
Field	1) Keyboard shift

This keyword defines the keyboard shift to be used in a display file or DFU when the field is referenced. REFSHIFT has no effect on the physical file itself. This keyword is allowed only for character (data type A) and numeric (data types S, B, and P) fields.

For a more complete explanation of keyboard shifts, see Chapter 3.

PARAMETER DEFINITION

Keyboard shift

This parameter specifies a valid keyboard shift for the field. The values allowed depend on the data type (coded in column 35).

Type of Field	Valid Values
Character field	A, X, W, N, I, D, M
Numeric field	S, Y, N, I, D

```
....1....+....2....+....3....+....4....+....5....+....6....+....7....+....8
A             R CUSFMT
A               CUSNBR         7P Ø         REFSHIFT(Y)
A               CUSNAM        35A
```

SIGNED (Signed)

Level	Parameters
Key	None

This keyword tells the AS/400 to take into consideration the sign of a numeric field (positive and negative values) when creating the index for the physical file.

```
....1....+....2....+....3....+....4....+....5....+....6....+....7....+....8
A             R SLSFMT
A               CUSNBR         7P Ø
A               CUSNAM        35A
A               ORDNBR         7P Ø
A               SLSAMT         9P 2
A             K SLSAMT                      SIGNED
```

TEXT (Text)

Level	Parameters
Record	1) Description
Field	

This keyword adds descriptive text to record formats or fields. The text serves as documentation only.

PARAMETER DEFINITION

Description
This parameter is a text field that can be up to 50 characters long and must be enclosed in apostrophes.

```
....1....+....2....+....3....+....4....+....5....+....6....+....7....+....8
A             R SLSFMT                      TEXT('Sales record format')
A               CUSNBR        7P 0           TEXT('Customer number')
A               CUSNAM        35A            TEXT('Customer name')
```

TIMFMT (Time Format)

Level	Parameters
Field	1) Time format

This keyword specifies the format of a time field (data type T). The length of the time field is always eight characters, regardless of the format specified.

PARAMETER DEFINITION

Time format
This parameter is one of the following codes, each of which represents a specific format for a time field.

Code	Meaning	Format
*HMS	Hours:minutes:seconds	hh:mm:ss
*ISO	International Standards Organization	hh.mm.ss
*USA	USA standard	hh:mm AM or hh:mm PM
*EUR	European standard	hh.mm.ss
*JIS	Japanese standard	hh:mm:ss

The default value for this keyword is *ISO.

```
....1....+....2....+....3....+....4....+....5....+....6....+....7....+....8
A             R CUSFMT
A               CUSNBR        7P 0
A               CUSNAM        35A
A               ENTTIM         T             TIMFMT(*HMS)
```

TIMSEP (Time Separator)

Level	Parameters
Field	1) Time separator

This keyword defines the separator to be used for a time field (data type L). If the time field is defined as *ISO, *USA, *EUR, or *JIS, you cannot specify this keyword.

PARAMETER DEFINITION

Time separator

This parameter is either an explicit value defined within apostrophes (') or a value of *JOB. The valid values are colon (:), period (.), and blank ( ). *JOB indicates that the job's default value is to be used.

```
....1....+....2....+....3....+....4....+....5....+....6....+....7....+....8
A              R CUSFMT
A                CUSNBR        7P 0
A                CUSNAM       35A
A                ENTTIM         T         TIMFMT(*HMS)
A                                         TIMSEP(':')
```

UNIQUE (Unique)

Level	Parameters
File	1) Null inclusion (optional)

This keyword tells the AS/400 that duplicate keys are not allowed for the index created for the physical file.

PARAMETER DEFINITION

Null inclusion

This optional parameter indicates whether null-value keys are to be considered when creating the index for the physical file. The valid values are *INCNULL and *EXCNULL. The default is *INCNULL. If you specify *INCNULL and two keys have null values, the result is a duplicate key.

```
....1....+....2....+....3....+....4....+....5....+....6....+....7....+....8
A                                         UNIQUE
A              R CUSFMT
A                CUSNBR        7P 0
A                CUSNAM       35A
A              K CUSNBR
```

UNSIGNED (Unsigned)

Level	Parameters
Key	None

This keyword tells the AS/400 to treat numeric fields as a string of binary data, not as numbers, when creating the index for the physical file.

```
....1....+....2....+....3....+....4....+....5....+....6....+....7....+....8
A              R SLSFMT
A                CUSNBR         7P 0
A                CUSNAM        35A
A                ORDNBR         7P 0
A                SLSAMT         9P 2
A              K SLSAMT                        UNSIGNED
```

VALUES (Values)

Level	Parameters
Field	1) Value 1; Value 2 ...Value 100 (optional)

This keyword does not affect the physical file itself. When a display file references the physical file field, the VALUES keyword is copied to provide default validity checking. For more information about how this keyword affects the screen field, see the VALUES keyword in the Display Files section of this guide.

PARAMETER DEFINITION

Value 1; Value 2 ... Value 100
You can specify up to 100 values to be checked against the field's value. The specified values must be of the same type as the field definition (e.g., a number for numeric fields, a character for character fields).

```
....1....+....2....+....3....+....4....+....5....+....6....+....7....+....8
A              R CUSFMT
A                CUSNBR         7P 0
A                CUSNAM        35A
A                CUSTER         3P 0      VALUES(2 3 5 100 250 278 765 999)
```

VARLEN (Variable Length Field)

Level	Parameters
Field	1) Allocated length (optional)

This keyword tells the AS/400 that the field is to be created as a variable-length field. VARLEN is valid only for character fields.

PARAMETER DEFINITION

Allocated length

This optional parameter is the minimum amount of storage the field will take up in the file. You can specify a number from 1 to the length defined for the field.

```
....1....+....2....+....3....+....4....+....5....+....6....+....7....+....8
A             R NOTEFMT
A               ORDNBR        7P 0
A               NOTE        1000A              VARLEN(32)
```

ZONE (Zone)

Level	Parameters
Key	None

This keyword tells the AS/400 to specify that only the zone portion (the left-most four bits) of every byte in the field is to be used to build the index for the physical file. The digit portion of the field is set to zero. This keyword is valid for character, hexadecimal, and zoned-decimal fields (data types A, H, and S).

```
....1....+....2....+....3....+....4....+....5....+....6....+....7....+....8
A             R SLSFMT
A               CUSNBR        7P 0
A               CUSNAM       35A
A               ORDNBR        7P 0
A               SLSAMT        9P 2
A             K CUSNAM                         ZONE
```

Chapter 2

Logical Files

When you create a logical file, you create an index over one or more physical files. Logical files contain no data; they are merely an index to where the physical data records reside.

TYPES OF LOGICAL FILES

You must keep in mind that there are three types of logical files:

- single-format
- multiple-format
- join

In a single-format logical file, one record format is defined, and that format applies to a single physical file.

A multiple-format logical file is one in which more than one record format is defined. Each record format can apply to the same file or to different files.

A join-logical file is one in which multiple physical file records are joined into a single record format. Records retrieved from join-logical files cannot be updated.

DATA TYPES

You specify a data type on a logical file only when you wish to override the data type from the physical file. The following table shows the valid data types (coded in column 35) for logical files:

Code	Meaning
Blank	Use data type from physical file
P	Packed decimal
S	Zoned decimal
B	Binary
F	Floating point
A	Character
H	Hexadecimal
L	Date
T	Time
Z	Timestamp

FIELD USAGE

The following table lists the field usages (column 38) available for logical files.

Code	Meaning
Blank	Both input and output; input only if a join-logical file
B	Both input and output; not valid for a join-logical file
I	Input only
N	Neither input nor output; valid for join-logical file only

KEYWORD LEVELS

You can specify keywords at five distinct levels for logical files:

- file level
- record-format level
- field level
- key level
- select/omit level

File level refers to keywords that affect the entire logical file. These keywords are coded before the first record format in the DDS source.

Record-format level refers to keywords that affect the format of the logical file. These keywords are placed before the first field defined within a record format. You define a record format by placing an R in column 17 of the A-spec.

Field level refers to those keywords that affect an individual field within the record format.

Key level refers to keywords specified on fields defined as being part of the key (index) for the logical file. You define a key field by placing a K in column 17 of the A-spec.

Select/omit level refers to keywords specified on any selection criteria you might have placed on an index for the logical file. You define select/omit statements by placing an S or an O in column 17 of the A-spec.

Join level is valid only for join-logical files and refers to keywords used to specify how files are joined together. You define a join specification by placing a J in column 17 of the A-spec. Join specifications are placed between the record-format-level keywords and the first field definition in the record format.

KEYWORDS

ABSVAL (Absolute Value)

Level	Parameters
Key	None

This keyword tells the AS/400 to ignore the sign of a numeric field when creating an index for the logical file — in other words, to treat negative numbers as positive numbers for index purposes. The database value remains negative.

```
....1....+....2....+....3....+....4....+....5....+....6....+....7....+....8
A          R SLSFMT                       PFILE(SALESHST)
A            CUSNBR
A            CUSNAM
A            ORDNBR
A            SLSAMT
A          K SLSAMT                        ABSVAL
```

ALIAS (Alternative Name)

Level	Parameters
Field	1) Alternate name

This keyword lets you assign a name longer than 10 characters for a field. If your HLL program allows for longer field names, this alias definition is used; otherwise, it is ignored.

PARAMETER DEFINITION

Alternate name

The alternate name specified can be up to 30 characters long.

```
....1....+....2....+....3....+....4....+....5....+....6....+....7....+....8
A          R CUSFMT                       PFILE(CUSTMAST)
A            CUSNBR                        ALIAS(CUSTOMER_NUMBER)
A            CUSNAM                        ALIAS(CUSTOMER_NAME)
```

ALL (All)

Level	Parameters
Select	None

This keyword specifies the action to be taken after all other select/omit specifications have been processed. You enter this keyword on a select/omit line with no field name.

```
....1....+....2....+....3....+....4....+....5....+....6....+....7....+....8
A          R SLSFMT                       PFILE(SALESHST)
A            CUSNBR
A            CUSNAM
A            ORDNBR
A            SLSAMT
A          K SLSAMT
A          S SLSAMT                        COMP(GT 1000)
A          O                               ALL
```

ALTSEQ (Alternate Collating Sequence)

Level	Parameters
File	1) Table name

This keyword tells the AS/400 to use an alternate sequencing table when creating the index for the logical file.

PARAMETER DEFINITION

Table name

This parameter is the name of the alternate collating-sequence table to be used. You can qualify the table name with the name of the library if you wish, as in the second example below.

```
....1....+....2....+....3....+....4....+....5....+....6....+....7....+....8
A                                        ALTSEQ(UPPERCASE)
A          R CUSFMT                       PFILE(CUSTMAST)
A            CUSNBR
A            CUSNAM
A          K CUSNAM
....1....+....2....+....3....+....4....+....5....+....6....+....7....+....8
A                                        ALTSEQ(PRODLIB/UPPERCASE)
A          R CUSFMT                       PFILE(CUSTMAST)
A            CUSNBR
A            CUSNAM
A          K CUSNAM
```

CCSID (Coded Character Set Identifier)

Level	Parameters
File Field	1) Value
	2) Field display length (optional)

This keyword lets you specify the number of the coded character set to be used for character fields in the physical file. When you specify CCSID at the file level, all character fields are affected; otherwise, only those fields containing CCSID are affected.

PARAMETER DEFINITIONS

Value

This parameter is a number up to five digits long that corresponds to a specific coded character set. For a list of valid codes, see IBM's *National Language Support* book.

Field Display Length

This optional parameter lets you define the displayable length of the field on a
screen when the field is referenced on a display.

```
....1....+....2....+....3....+....4....+....5....+....6....+....7....+....8
A                                      CCSID(37)
A            R CUSFMT                  PFILE(CUSTOMER)
....1....+....2....+....3....+....4....+....5....+....6....+....7....+....8
A                                      CCSID(37)
A            R CUSFMT                  PFILE(CUSTOMER)
A              CUSNBR    R
A              CUSNAM    R             CCSID(500 30)
A              CUSAD1    R
```

CHECK (Check)

Level	Parameters
Field	1) Edit check code

This keyword does not affect the logical file itself. When a display file references
the logical file field on which you've coded the CHECK keyword, the keyword
is copied to provide default validity checking. See the CHECK keyword in the
Display Files section of this guide for more information about how CHECK
affects the screen field.

Parameter Definition

Edit check code

This parameter is a character code that must be one of the following values:

Code	Meaning
AB	Allow blank
ME	Mandatory enter
MF	Mandatory fill
M10	Modulus 10 self-check
M10F	Modulus 10 self-check
M11	Modulus 11 self-check
M11F	Modulus 11 self-check
VN	Validate name
VNE	Validate name extended

You can specify more than one code in the CHECK keyword.

```
....1....+....2....+....3....+....4....+....5....+....6....+....7....+....8
A            R CUSFMT                  PFILE(CUSTMAST)
A              CUSNBR                  CHECK(M10 MF)
A              CUSNAM                  CHECK(ME)
A              CUSAD1
```

CHKMSGID (Check Message Identifier)

Level	Parameters
Field	1) Message ID
	2) Message file
	3) Message data field (optional)

This keyword lets you specify a particular message ID to be used with the validity-checking keyword specified on the field. The specified message ID is used instead of the AS/400's default message.

When you reference this field in a display file, the CHKMSGID keyword is copied to the display file. You can specify CHKMSGID only when you use one of the following keywords: VALUES, RANGE, CMP, COMP, CHECK(M10), CHECK(M11), CHECK(VN), or CHECK(VNE).

PARAMETER DEFINITIONS

Message ID

This parameter is a seven-character identifier for the message to be used.

Message file

This parameter is the name of the file in which the message ID is located. You can qualify the file name with the library if you wish, as in the second example below.

Message data field

This optional parameter specifies the name of a field that contains data the message ID uses to format the message text properly. See the CHKMSGID keyword in Chapter 3 for more information about how this parameter works.

```
....1....+....2....+....3....+....4....+....5....+....6....+....7....+....8
A          R CUSFMT              PFILE(CUSTMAST)
A            CUSNBR
A            CUSNAM
A            RATING               RANGE(1 5)
A                                 CHKMSGID(USR0001 USERMSGF)
....1....+....2....+....3....+....4....+....5....+....6....+....7....+....8
A          R CUSFMT              PFILE(CUSTMAST)
A            CUSNBR
A            CUSNAM
A            RATING               RANGE(1 5)
A                                 CHKMSGID(USR0001 PRODLIB/USERMSGF +
                                 &DATA)
```

CMP (Comparison)

Level	Parameters
Field	1) Relational operator
	2) Value

This keyword is the same as the COMP keyword. You should use the COMP keyword instead, however, as the CMP keyword exists simply for backward compatibility.

COLHDG (Column Heading)

Level	Parameters
Field	Line 1
	Line 2 (optional)
	Line 3 (optional)

This keyword lets you specify up to three lines of text to be used as a column heading for the field. Many IBM utilities that allow data manipulation or listing in a logical file (e.g., Query/400, DFU) select these headings.

PARAMETER DEFINITIONS

Line 1
This parameter specifies up to 20 characters of text contained within apostrophes (').

Line 2
This parameter specifies up to 20 characters of text contained within apostrophes (').

Line 3
This parameter specifies up to 20 characters of text contained within apostrophes (').

```
....1....+....2....+....3....+....4....+....5....+....6....+....7....+....8
A           R SLSFMT                    PFILE(SALESHST)
A             CUSNBR                    COLHDG('Customer' 'Number')
A             CUSNAM                    COLHDG('Customer' 'Name')
A             ORDNBR                    COLHDG('Order' 'Number')
A             SLSAMT                    COLHDG('Total' 'Sales' 'Amount')
```

COMP (Comparison)

Level	Parameters
Field Select	1) Relational operator
	2) Value

When you specify this keyword at the field level, it has no effect on the logical file. When a display file references the logical file field, the COMP keyword is copied to provide default validity checking.

When you specify this keyword at the select/omit level, it is used to define a comparison test to determine whether a record should be included or excluded from the index.

PARAMETER DEFINITIONS

Relational operator

This parameter is a two-character code that specifies the type of comparison test to be performed.

Operator	Meaning
EQ	Equal to
NE	Not equal to
LT	Less than
NL	Not less than
GT	Greater than
NG	Not greater than
LE	Less than or equal to
GE	Greater than or equal to

Value

This parameter is the specific value to be tested against. The value entered must be in the same format as the field definition.

For select/omit specifications, you can also specify a field name or *NULL for the value test. For *NULL, the relational operator must be EQ or NE.

```
....1....+....2....+....3....+....4....+....5....+....6....+....7....+....8
A          R SLSFMT                    PFILE(SALESHST)
A            CUSNBR
A            CUSNAM                     COMP(NE ' ')
A            ORDNBR                     COMP(GT 0)
A            ORDQTY
A            SHPQTY
A            SLSAMT                     COMP(GE 0)
A          K SLSAMT
A          S SLSAMT                     COMP(GT 1000)
A            SHPQTY                     COMP(GT ORDQTY)
```

CONCAT (Concatenate)

Level	Parameters
Field	1) Field 1; Field 2; Field 3.....

This keyword lets you take two or more physical-file field names and concatenate them into a single field in the logical file. You must specify at least two fields; the maximum number of fields allowed depends on the length of the result field.

PARAMETER DEFINITION

Field 1; Field 2; Field 3 ...
For this parameter, the field names provided must exist in the referenced physical file.

```
....1....+....2....+....3....+....4....+....5....+....6....+....7....+....8
A           R CUSFMT                     PFILE(CUSTMAST)
A             CUSNBR
A             CUSNAM
A             CUSAD1
A             CUSCTY
A             CUSSTA
A             CUSZIP
A             ZIPLIN        60           CONCAT(CUSCTY CUSSTA CUSZIP)
```

DATFMT (Date Format)

Level	Parameters
Field	1) Date format

This keyword lets you change the format of a date field in the physical file.

PARAMETER DEFINITION

Date format
This parameter is a code that specifies the format of a date field. The table below shows all valid values.

Code	Meaning	Format	Length
*JOB	Job default	Depends on job	—
*MDY	Month/day/year	mm/dd/yy	8
*DMY	Day/month/year	dd/mm/yy	8
*YMD	Year/month/day	yy/mm/dd	8
*JUL	Julian	yy/ddd	6
*ISO	International Standards Organization	yyyy-mm-dd	10
*USA	USA Standard	mm/dd/yyyy	10
*EUR	European Standard	dd.mm.yyyy	10
*JIS	Japanese Standard	yyyy-mm-dd	10

The default value for this parameter is the same as that specified on the physical file.

```
....1....+....2....+....3....+....4....+....5....+....6....+....7....+....8
A           R CUSFMT                     PFILE(CUSTMAST)
A             CUSNBR
A             CUSNAM
A             ENTDTE                     DATFMT(*JUL)
```

DATSEP (Date Separator)

Level	Parameters
Field	1) Date separator

This keyword lets you change the separator defined for a date field in the physical file.

PARAMETER DEFINITION

Date separator
This parameter is either an explicit value defined within apostrophes (') or a value of *JOB. The valid values are slash (/), dash (-), period (.), comma (,), and blank ( ). Special value *JOB indicates that the job's default separator is to be used.

```
....1....+....2....+....3....+....4....+....5....+....6....+....7....+....8
A             R CUSFMT                  PFILE(CUSTMAST)
A               CUSNBR
A               CUSNAM
A               ENTDTE                  DATFMT(*YMD)
A                                       DATSEP('.')
```

DESCEND (Descending Sequence)

Level	Parameters
Key	None

This keyword tells the AS/400 to sort the field in descending sequence when creating the index for the logical file.

```
....1....+....2....+....3....+....4....+....5....+....6....+....7....+....8
A             R SLSFMT                  PFILE(SALESHST)
A               CUSNBR
A               CUSNAM
A               ORDNBR
A               SLSAMT
A             K SLSAMT                  DESCEND
```

DIGIT (Digit)

Level	Parameters
Key	None

This keyword tells the AS/400 to use only the digit portion (the rightmost 4 bits) of each byte in a field to create the index for the logical file. The zone portion is set to zero. This keyword is valid for character, hexadecimal, and zoned-decimal fields (data types A, H, and S).

```
....1....+....2....+....3....+....4....+....5....+....6....+....7....+....8
A          R SLSFMT                       PFILE(SALESHST)
A            CUSNBR
A            CUSNAM
A            ORDNBR
A            SLSAMT
A          K CUSNAM                        DIGIT
```

DYNSLT (Dynamic Selection)

Level	Parameters
File	None

This keyword tells the AS/400 to perform select/omit testing for the index associated with the logical file at processing time (i.e., dynamically).

```
....1....+....2....+....3....+....4....+....5....+....6....+....7....+....8
A                                          DYNSLT
A          R SLSFMT                        PFILE(SALESHST)
A            CUSNBR
A            CUSNAM
A            ORDNBR
A            SLSAMT
A          K CUSNAM
A          S SLSAMT                        COMP(GT 1000)
```

EDTCDE (Edit Code)

Level	Parameters
Field	1) Edit code
	2) Floating character (optional)

This keyword does not affect the logical file itself. When a display file references the logical file field, the EDTCDE specified is copied to provide default screen editing of the field. See the EDTCDE keyword in Chapter 3 for a full discussion of the codes and how they look on the screen.

PARAMETER DEFINITIONS

Edit code
This parameter is a valid AS/400 edit code.

Floating character
This optional parameter is either an asterisk (*) or any other character selected to act as a floating currency symbol. An asterisk indicates that the numeric field is to have all leading zeros replaced with asterisks. The floating character appears to the left of the most significant digit.

```
....1....+....2....+....3....+....4....+....5....+....6....+....7....+....8
A               R SLSFMT                    PFILE(SALESHST)
A                 CUSNBR                    EDTCDE(4)
A                 CUSNAM
A                 ORDNBR                    EDTCDE(4)
A                 SLSAMT                    EDTCDE(L)
```

EDTWRD (Edit Word)

Level	Parameters
Key	1) Edit word

This keyword does not affect the logical file itself. When a display file references the logical file field, the specified EDTWRD is copied to provide default screen editing of the field. See the EDTWRD keyword in Chapter 3 for a full discussion of how to define an edit word.

PARAMETER DEFINITION

Edit word

This parameter is a valid AS/400 edit word character string.

```
....1....+....2....+....3....+....4....+....5....+....6....+....7....+....8
A               R PRSFMT                    PFILE(PAYMASTR)
A                 EMP#
A                 EMPNAM
A                 SSN                        EDTWRD('   -  -   ')
```

FCFO (First-Changed First-Out)

Level	Parameters
File	None

This keyword tells the AS/400 that when duplicate records exist in the index for the logical file, the record that was changed first is to be retrieved first.

You cannot specify this keyword with the keywords FIFO, LIFO, or UNIQUE.

```
....1....+....2....+....3....+....4....+....5....+....6....+....7....+....8
A                                           FCFO
A               R SLSFMT                    PFILE(SALESHST)
A                 CUSNBR
A                 CUSNAM
A                 ORDNBR
A                 SLSAMT
A               K SLSAMT
```

FIFO (First-In First-Out)

Level	Parameters
File	None

This keyword tells the AS/400 that when duplicate records exist in the index for the logical file, the record that was put into the file first is to be retrieved first.

You cannot specify this keyword with the keywords FCFO, LIFO, or UNIQUE.

```
....1....+....2....+....3....+....4....+....5....+....6....+....7....+....8
A                                       FIFO
A             R SLSFMT                   PFILE(SALESHST)
A               CUSNBR
A               CUSNAM
A               ORDNBR
A               SLSAMT
A             K SLSAMT
```

FLTPCN (Floating-Point Precision)

Level	Parameters
Field	1) Precision

This keyword defines the precision of a floating-point field (data type F).

PARAMETER DEFINITION

Precision
This parameter can have a value of either *SINGLE or *DOUBLE. Single-precision fields can be up to 9 digits long, whereas double-precision fields can be up to 17 digits long. The default is single precision.

```
....1....+....2....+....3....+....4....+....5....+....6....+....7....+....8
A             R SCIENCE                  PFILE(STATFILE)
A               CALC1                    FLTPCN(*DOUBLE)
A               CALC2                    FLTPCN(*SINGLE)
A               CALC3
```

FORMAT (Format)

Level	Parameters
Record	1) File name

This keyword references another database file on the AS/400 from which all the fields are to be shared. The record format name must exist in the other database file. This keyword is not valid for join-logical files.

PARAMETER DEFINITION

File name
This parameter is the name of the database file in which the format name is to be found. You can qualify the file name with the name of the library if you wish, as in the second example below.

```
....1....+....2....+....3....+....4....+....5....+....6....+....7....+....8
A           R SLSFMT                        FORMAT(SALESHST)
```

```
....1....+....2....+....3....+....4....+....5....+....6....+....7....+....8
A           R SLSFMT                        FORMAT(PRODLIB/SALESHST)
```

JDFTVAL (Join Default Values) (Join-Logical File Only)

Level	Parameters
File	None

This keyword tells the AS/400 that when records are joined, if a join to a secondary record does not occur, the system is to provide default values for fields retrieved from the secondary file. If you don't specify this keyword, records in the primary file are skipped if there is no corresponding record in the secondary file (see the discussion of the JFLD keyword).

```
....1....+....2....+....3....+....4....+....5....+....6....+....7....+....8
A                                           JDFTVAL
A           R RECORD1                       JFILE(ORDERMST CUSTMAST)
A           J                               JOIN(ORDERMST CUSTMAST)
A                                           JFLD(CUST# CUSNBR)
A             CUSNBR
A             CUSNAM
A             ORDNBR
A             SLSAMT
A           K SLSAMT
```

JDUPSEQ (Join Duplicate Sequence) (Join-Logical File Only)

Level	Parameters
Join	1) Sequencing field
	2) Descending (optional)

This keyword specifies the order in which duplicate records are arranged for a join-logical file. You can specify more than one JDUPSEQ keyword per join. The order of the JDUPSEQ keywords determines the order in which duplicate records are presented.

PARAMETER DEFINITIONS

Sequencing field
This parameter is the name of a field within the record format of the join-logical file.

Descending
This is an optional parameter to specify that the sequencing field should be in descending sequence. Use a value of *DESCEND to specify descending sequence. The default is ascending sequence.

```
....1....+....2....+....3....+....4....+....5....+....6....+....7....+....8
A                                        JDFTVAL
A              R RECORD1                 JFILE(ORDERMST CUSTMAST)
A              J                         JOIN(ORDERMST CUSTMAST)
A                                        JFLD(CUST# CUSNBR)
A                                        JDUPSEQ(ORDNBR)
A                CUSNBR
A                CUSNAM
A                ORDNBR
A                SLSAMT
A              K SLSAMT
```

JFILE (Joined Files) (Join-Logical File Only)

Level	Parameters
Record	1) Physical file name; Physical file name 2 ... Physical file name 32

This keyword specifies all the physical files to be used to make up the join-logical file. The first file specified is considered the primary file; all others are considered secondary.

This keyword does not specify how to join the files (refer to the discussion of the JFLD keyword for that information).

PARAMETER DEFINITION

Physical file name

This parameter is the name of the physical file to be joined. You can join up to 32 files. You can qualify the file name with the library name if you wish.

```
....1....+....2....+....3....+....4....+....5....+....6....+....7....+....8
A                                        JDFTVAL
A              R RECORD1                 JFILE(ORDERMST CUSTMAST)
A              J                         JOIN(ORDERMST CUSTMAST)
A                                        JFLD(CUST# CUSNBR)
A                CUSNBR
A                CUSNAM
A                ORDNBR
A                SLSAMT
A              K SLSAMT
```

JFLD (Joined Fields) (Join-Logical File Only)

Level	Parameters
Join	1) From field name
	2) To field name

This keyword specifies how physical files are to be joined together. You must code at least one JFLD keyword for every specified JOIN keyword. You can think of JFLD as a CHAIN operation; the order in which you specify the JFLD keywords determines the order in which the files are linked.

PARAMETER DEFINITIONS

From field name

This parameter is the name of a field found in the first file specified in the JOIN keyword.

To field name

This parameter is the name of a field found in the second file specified in the JOIN keyword.

The specified fields must have the same attributes (length, data type, decimal positions).

```
....1....+....2....+....3....+....4....+....5....+....6....+....7....+....8
A                                        JDFTVAL
A          R RECORD1                     JFILE(ORDERMST CUSTMAST)
A          J                             JOIN(ORDERMST CUSTMAST)
A                                        JFLD(CUST# CUSNBR)
A            CUSNBR
A            CUSNAM
A            ORDNBR
A            SLSAMT
A          K SLSAMT
```

JOIN (Join) (Join-Logical File Only)

Level	Parameters
Join	1) From file
	2) To file

This keyword specifies the names of two physical files to be joined. You specify the join level on this keyword (J in column 17). You can specify only two files with this keyword; to join more than two files, code as many JOIN keywords as you need to link all the files.

PARAMETER DEFINITIONS

From file

This parameter is the name of the first file to be joined. If you wish, you can specify a relative position number instead of the file name. The relative position number corresponds to the position of the file in the JFILE keyword.

To file

This parameter specifies the name of the second file to be joined. If you wish, you can specify a relative position number instead of the file name. The relative position number corresponds to the position of the file in the JFILE keyword.

```
....1....+....2....+....3....+....4....+....5....+....6....+....7....+....8
A                                         JDFTVAL
A          R RECORD1                      JFILE(ORDERMST CUSTMAST)
A          J                              JOIN(ORDERMST CUSTMAST)
A                                         JFLD(CUST# CUSNBR)
A            CUSNBR
A            CUSNAM
A            ORDNBR
A            SLSAMT
A          K SLSAMT
....1....+....2....+....3....+....4....+....5....+....6....+....7....+....8
A                                         JDFTVAL
A          R RECORD1                      JFILE(ORDERMST CUSTMAST ITEMMAST)
A          J                              JOIN(1 2)
A                                         JFLD(CUST# CUSNBR)
A          J                              JOIN(1 3)
A                                         JFLD(ITEM# PART#)
A            CUSNBR
A            CUSNAM
A            ORDNBR
A            ITEM#
A            SLSAMT
A          K SLSAMT
```

JREF (Join Reference) (Join-Logical File Only)

Level	Parameters
Field	1) File name

This keyword qualifies the name of the file from which a field is to be retrieved. Use this keyword when a field appears in more than one of the files specified on the JFILE keyword.

PARAMETER DEFINITION

File name
This parameter is the name of the file from which the field is to be retrieved. If you wish, you can specify a relative position number instead of the file name. The relative position number corresponds to the position of the file in the JFILE keyword.

```
....1....+....2....+....3....+....4....+....5....+....6....+....7....+....8
A                                         JDFTVAL
A          R RECORD1                      JFILE(ORDERMST CUSTMAST)
A          J                              JOIN(ORDERMST CUSTMAST)
A                                         JFLD(CUSNBR CUSNBR)
A            CUSNBR                       JREF(ORDERMST)
A            CUSNAM
A            ORDNBR
A            SLSAMT
A          K SLSAMT
```

```
....1....+....2....+....3....+....4....+....5....+....6....+....7....+....8
A                                            JDFTVAL
A          R RECORD1                         JFILE(ORDERMST CUSTMAST ITEMMAST)
A          J                                 JOIN(1 2)
A                                            JFLD(CUSNBR CUSNBR)
A          J                                 JOIN(1 3)
A                                            JFLD(ITEM# ITEM#)
A            CUSNBR                           JFLD(1)
A            CUSNAM
A            ORDNBR
A            ITEM#                            JFLD(3)
A            SLSAMT
A          K SLSAMT
```

LIFO (Last-In First-Out)

Level	Parameters
File	None

This keyword tells the AS/400 that when duplicate records exist in the index for the logical file, the record that was put into the file last is to be retrieved first.

You cannot specify this keyword with the keywords FCFO, FIFO, or UNIQUE.

```
....1....+....2....+....3....+....4....+....5....+....6....+....7....+....8
A                                            LIFO
A          R SLSFMT                          PFILE(SALESHST)
A            CUSNBR
A            CUSNAM
A            ORDNBR
A            SLSAMT
A          K SLSAMT
```

NOALTSEQ (No Alternate Collating Sequence)

Level	Paramters
Key	None

This keyword lets you override the effect of the file-level ALTSEQ keyword. When you specify this keyword, the key field is not sequenced by the table specified in the ALTSEQ keyword.

```
....1....+....2....+....3....+....4....+....5....+....6....+....7....+....8
A                                            ALTSEQ(UPPERCASE)
A          R CUSFMT                          PFILE(CUSTMAST)
A            CUSNBR
A            CUSNAM
A            CUSAD1
A            CUSCTY
A            CUSSTA
A          K CUSSTA                          NOALTSEQ
A          K CUSCTY                          NOALTSEQ
A          K CUSNAM
```

PFILE (Physical File)

Level	Parameters
Record	1) Physical file; Physical file 2 ... Physical file 32

This keyword identifies the names of the physical files that contain the data being accessed through the record format. This keyword is required for every record format in a single- or multiple-format logical file. PFILE is not allowed with join logical files. Under most circumstances, you specify only one physical file name.

PARAMETER DEFINITION

Physical file
This parameter contains the name of the physical file or files for which data is accessed. You can specify up to 32 file names. You can qualify the file name with the name of the library if you wish.

```
....1....+....2....+....3....+....4....+....5....+....6....+....7....+....8
A              R CUSFMT                      PFILE(CUSTMAST)
A                CUSNBR
A                CUSNAM
A                CUSAD1
A                CUSCTY
A                CUSSTA
A              K CUSSTA
A              K CUSCTY
A              K CUSNAM
```

RANGE (Range)

Level	Parameters
Field	1) Low value
Select	1) High value

Specifying this keyword at the field level does not affect the logical file itself. When a display file references this logical file field, the RANGE keyword is copied to provide default validity checking.

When you specify this keyword at the select/omit level, it instructs the AS/400 whether to include or exclude records in the index based on the range of values entered.

PARAMETER DEFINITIONS

Low value
This parameter is the lower end of the valid range for the field. The value entered must be of the same type as the field definition (e.g., a number for numeric fields, a character for character fields).

High value

This parameter is the upper end of the valid range for the field. The value entered must be of the same type as the field definition.

The low and high values are included in the valid values for the field.

```
....1....+....2....+....3....+....4....+....5....+....6....+....7....+....8
A              R CUSFMT                    PFILE(CUSTMAST)
A                CUSNBR
A                CUSNAM
A                CUSTER                    RANGE(1 150)
A              K CUSNBR
A              S CUSTER                    RANGE(1 10)
```

REFACCPTH (Reference Access Path Definition)

Level	Parameters
File	1) Database file name

This keyword specifies that the access path (index) is to be copied from another database file index. You may not specify a key or any select/omit information when you use keyword REFACCPTH.

PARAMETER DEFINITION

Database file name

This parameter is the name of the database file from which the access path is to be copied. If you wish, you can qualify the file name with the name of the library in which the database file is located.

```
....1....+....2....+....3....+....4....+....5....+....6....+....7....+....8
A                                          REFACCPTH(SALESL3)
A              R SLSFMT                    PFILE(SALESHST)
A                CUSNBR
A                CUSNAM
A                CUSAD1
```

REFSHIFT (Reference Shift)

Level	Parameters
Field	1) Keyboard shift

This keyword defines the keyboard shift to be used in a display file or DFU when the field is referenced. REFSHIFT has no effect on the logical file itself. This keyword is allowed only for character (data type A) and numeric (data types S, B, and P) fields.

For an explanation of keyboard shifts, see the discussion of data types near the beginning of Chapter 3.

PARAMETER DEFINITION

Keyboard shift

This parameter specifies a valid keyboard shift for the field. The valid values allowed depend on the data type (column 35).

Type of Field	Valid Values
Character field	A, X, W, N, I, D, M
Numeric field	S, Y, N, I, D

```
....1....+....2....+....3....+....4....+....5....+....6....+....7....+....8
A          R CUSFMT                    PFILE(CUSTMAST)
A            CUSNBR                     REFSHIFT(Y)
A            CUSNAM
```

RENAME (Rename)

Level	Parameters
Field	1) Field name

This keyword gives a field another name.

PARAMETER DEFINITION

Field name

This parameter specifies the new name to give the field.

```
....1....+....2....+....3....+....4....+....5....+....6....+....7....+....8
A          R CUSFMT                    PFILE(CUSTMAST)
A            CUST#                      RENAME(CUSNBR)
A            CUSNAM
```

SIGNED (Signed)

Level	Parameters
Key	None

This keyword tells the AS/400 to take into consideration the sign of a numeric field (positive and negative values) when creating the index for the logical file.

```
....1....+....2....+....3....+....4....+....5....+....6....+....7....+....8
A          R SLSFMT                    PFILE(SALESHST)
A            CUSNBR
A            CUSNAM
A            ORDNBR
A            SLSAMT
A          K SLSAMT                     SIGNED
```

SST (Substring)

Level	Parameters
Field	1) Field name
	2) Starting position
	3) Length (optional)

This keyword extracts a character-string subset of an existing field. You can specify this keyword only on character, hexadecimal, and zoned-decimal fields (data types A, H, and S).

PARAMETER DEFINITIONS

Field name

This parameter is the name of the field from which the character string is to be extracted. This field name must be specified in the logical-file record format and before the SST keyword definition.

Starting position

This parameter is a number indicating the position at which to start extracting the character string. The parameter value cannot exceed the length of the field.

Length

This optional parameter specifies how many characters to extract. If you don't specify a length, everything from the starting position to the end of the field is extracted. The starting position plus the length cannot exceed the length of the field.

```
....1....+....2....+....3....+....4....+....5....+....6....+....7....+....8
A           R SLSFMT                    PFILE(SALESHST)
A             CUSNBR
A             CUSNAM
A             SHRTNM        10           SST(CUSNAM 1 10)
A             ORDNBR
A             SLSAMT
```

TEXT (Text)

Level	Parameters
Record Field	1) Description

This keyword adds descriptive text to record formats or fields. The text serves as documentation only.

PARAMETER DEFINITION

Description

This parameter is a text field up to 50 characters long enclosed in apostrophes.

```
....1....+....2....+....3....+....4....+....5....+....6....+....7....+....8
A          R SLSFMT                      PFILE(SALESHST)
A                                        TEXT('Sales record format')
A            CUSNBR                      TEXT('Customer number')
A            CUSNAM                      TEXT('Customer name')
```

TIMFMT (Time Format)

Level	Parameters
Field	1) Time format

This keyword overrides the time format for a time field in the physical file.

PARAMETER DEFINITION

Time format
This parameter is a code that represents the format of a time field.

Code	Meaning	Format
*HMS	Hours:minutes:seconds	hh:mm:ss
*ISO	International Standards Organization	hh.mm.ss
*USA	USA standard	hh:mm Amor hh:mm PM
*EUR	European standard	hh.mm.ss
*JIS	Japanese standard	hh:mm:ss

The default value for this parameter is the same time format as the physical file field.

```
....1....+....2....+....3....+....4....+....5....+....6....+....7....+....8
A          R CUSFMT                      PFILE(CUSTMAST)
A            CUSNBR
A            CUSNAM
A            ENTTIM                      TIMFMT(*USA)
```

TIMSEP (Time Separator)

Level	Parameters
Field	1) Time separator

This keyword overrides the time separator for the physical file time field.

PARAMETER DEFINITION

Time separator
This parameter is either an explicit value defined within apostrophes (') or a special value of *JOB. The valid values are colon (:), period (.), and blank ( ). Special value *JOB indicates the job's default time separator is to be used.

```
....1....+....2....+....3....+....4....+....5....+....6....+....7....+....8
A          R CUSFMT                        PFILE(CUSTMAST)
A            CUSNBR
A            CUSNAM
A            ENTTIM                         TIMFMT(*HMS)
A                                           TIMSEP(':')
```

TRNTBL (Translation Table)

Level	Parameters
Field	1) File name

This keyword specifies the name of the translation table used to convert the field data in the physical file before passing the field to your HLL program. This keyword is valid for input-only fields (data usage I or N).

PARAMETER DEFINITION

File name

This parameter specifies the name of the translation table to be used. You can qualify the table name with the library name if you wish.

```
....1....+....2....+....3....+....4....+....5....+....6....+....7....+....8
A          R CUSFMT                        PFILE(CUSTMAST)
A            CUSNBR
A            CUSNAM          I              TRNTBL(PRODLIB/TRANSTBL)
```

UNIQUE (Unique)

Level	Parameters
File	1) Null inclusion (optional)

This keyword tells the AS/400 that duplicate keys are not allowed for the index created for this logical file.

PARAMETER DEFINITION

Null inclusion

The optional parameter indicates whether null-value keys are to be considered when the index is created for the logical file. The valid values are *INCNULL and *EXCNULL. The default is *INCNULL, which results in a duplicate key if two keys have null values.

```
....1....+....2....+....3....+....4....+....5....+....6....+....7....+....8
A                                           UNIQUE
A          R CUSFMT                         PFILE(CUSTMAST)
A            CUSNBR
A            CUSNAM
A          K CUSNBR
```

UNSIGNED (Unsigned)

Level	Parameters
Key	None

This keyword tells the AS/400 to treat numeric fields as a string of binary data, not as numbers, when creating the index for the logical file.

```
....1....+....2....+....3....+....4....+....5....+....6....+....7....+....8
A           R SLSFMT              PFILE(SALESHST)
A             CUSNBR
A             CUSNAM
A             ORDNBR
A             SLSAMT
A           K SLSAMT              UNSIGNED
```

VALUES (Values)

Level	Parameters
Field	
Select	1) Value 1; Value 2 ...Value 100 (Optional)

When a display file references the logical file field, the VALUES keyword is copied to provide default validity checking. At the select/omit level, the keyword affects how records are included or excluded from the index created for the logical file.

Specifying the VALUES keyword at the field level has no effect at the file level.

PARAMETER DEFINITION

Value n

You can specify up to 100 values to be checked for the field. The value entered must be of the same type as the field definition (e.g., a number for numeric fields, a character for character fields).

```
....1....+....2....+....3....+....4....+....5....+....6....+....7....+....8
A           R CUSFMT              PFILE(CUSTMAST)
A             CUSNBR
A             CUSNAM
A             CUSTER              VALUES(2 3 5 100 250 278 765 999)
A           K CUSNBR
A           S CUSTER              VALUES(5 250)
```

VARLEN (Variable Length Field)

Level	Parameters
Field	1) Allocated length (optional)

This keyword tells the AS/400 that the field is to be created as a variable-length field. VARLEN is valid only for character fields.

PARAMETER DEFINITION

Allocated length

This optional parameter specifies the minimum amount of storage the field will occupy in the file. The parameter value can be a number from 1 to the length of the field.

```
....1....+....2....+....3....+....4....+....5....+....6....+....7....+....8
A          R NOTEFMT                      PFILE(NOTEFILE)
A            ORDNBR
A            NOTE                          VARLEN(64)
```

ZONE (Zone)

Level	Parameters
Key	None

This keyword tells the AS/400 to specify that only the zone portion (the leftmost four bits) of every byte in the field is to be used when building the index for the logical file. The digit portion of the byte is set to zero. This keyword is valid for character, hexadecimal, and zoned-decimal fields (data types A, H, and S).

```
....1....+....2....+....3....+....4....+....5....+....6....+....7....+....8
A          R SLSFMT                       PFILE(SALESHST)
A            CUSNBR
A            CUSNAM
A            ORDNBR
A            SLSAMT
A          K CUSNAM                        ZONE
```

Chapter 3

Display Files

Display files let you define screen specifications external to your HLL program. This section of DDS is the most complex because of the sheer number of key-words available.

DATA TYPES

For the most part, data types for display files control what kind of data you can enter into an input-capable field. Data types are sometimes referred to as *keyboard shifts*. The following table shows the valid data types (coded in column 35) for display files.

Code	Meaning
Blank	Default
A	Alphanumeric
D	Digits only
F	Floating point
I	Inhibit keyboard entry
L	Date
M	Numeric-only character
N	Numeric shift
S	Signed numeric
T	Time
W	Katakana (Japanese only)
X	Alphabetic only
Y	Numeric only
Z	Timestamp

The default data type is A for character fields and S for numeric fields.

FIELD USAGE

The table below shows the field usages (coded in column 38) available for display files.

Code	Meaning
Blank	Output
B	Both input and output
H	Hidden
I	Input
M	Message
O	Output
P	Program-to-system field

KEYWORD LEVELS

Display files have four distinct levels at which you can specify keywords: file level, record-format level, field level, and help level.

A keyword specified at the file level affects the entire display file. You code file-level keywords before the first record format in the DDS source.

Record-format–level keywords affect a specific display file record format. You define a record format by placing an R in column 17 of the A-spec. Code record-format–level keywords before the first field definition in the record format.

Field-level keywords affect an individual field within the record format.

Help-level keywords define a help specification. You define a help specification by placing an H in column 17 of the A-spec. Code help-level keywords between the record-format–level keywords and the first field definition.

KEYWORDS

The Conditioning column in the table for each keyword indicates whether you can specify indicators in columns 7 through 16.

ALARM (Alarm)

Level	Conditioning	Parameters
Record	Yes	None

This keyword sounds an audible alarm at the workstation.

```
....1....+....2....+....3....+....4....+....5....+....6....+....7....+....8
A           R FORMAT1
A   40                                      ALARM
A             CUSNBR        7S 0   10 10
A             CUSNAM       35A     10 20
```

ALIAS (Alternative Name)

Level	Conditioning	Parameters
Field	No	1) Alternate name

This keyword lets you assign a name longer than 10 characters for a field. If your HLL program supports longer field names, this alias definition is used; otherwise, it is ignored.

PARAMETER DEFINITION

Alternate name
The alternate name specified can be up to 30 characters long.

```
....1....+....2....+....3....+....4....+....5....+....6....+....7....+....8
A              R FORMAT1
A                CUSNBR         7S 0   10 10ALIAS(CUSTOMER_NUMBER)
A                CUSNAM        35A     10 20ALIAS(CUSTOMER_NAME)
```

ALTHELP (Alternative Help Key)

Level	Conditioning	Parameters
File	No	1) Attention key (optional)

This keyword defines a command attention key (see the CAnn keyword) to act as the Help key. The Help key is still available.

PARAMETER DEFINITION

Attention key

The valid values for this parameter are CA01 through CA24. The default is CA01.

```
....1....+....2....+....3....+....4....+....5....+....6....+....7....+....8
A                                       ALTHELP(CA08)
A              R FORMAT1                 HELP
A                CUSNBR         7S 0   10 10
A                CUSNAM        35A     10 20
```

ALTNAME (Alternate Record Name)

Level	Conditioning	Parameters
Record	No	1) Alternate name

This keyword defines an alternate name for a record format. ALTNAME is used for display files running in the System/36 environment.

PARAMETER DEFINITION

Alternate name

This parameter is a name from one to eight characters long. The first character must not be an asterisk.

```
....1....+....2....+....3....+....4....+....5....+....6....+....7....+....8
A              R FORMAT1                 ALTNAME('R( 2).a')
```

ALTPAGEDWN (Alternate Page Down)

Level	Conditioning	Parameters
File	No	1) Function key (optional)

This keyword defines a command function key (refer to the CFnn keyword discussion) to act as the Page down or Roll up key. The user can use either the command function key or the actual page/roll key.

PARAMETER DEFINITION

Function key
The valid values for this parameter are CF01 through CF24. The default is CF08.

```
....1....+....2....+....3....+....4....+....5....+....6....+....7....+....8
A                                            ALTPAGEDWN(CF1Ø)
A          R FORMAT1                         ROLLUP
A            CUSNBR        7S Ø   1Ø 1Ø
A            CUSNAM        35A    1Ø 2Ø
```

ALTPAGEUP (Alternate Page Up)

Level	Conditioning	Parameters
File	No	1) Function key (optional)

This keyword defines a command function key (refer to the CFnn keyword discussion) to act as the Page up or Roll down key. The user can use either the command function key or the actual page/roll key.

PARAMETER DEFINITION

Function key
The valid values for this parameter are CF01 through CF24. The default is CF07.

```
....1....+....2....+....3....+....4....+....5....+....6....+....7....+....8
A                                            ALTPAGEUP(CF11)
A          R FORMAT1                         ROLLDOWN
A            CUSNBR        7S Ø   1Ø 1Ø
A            CUSNAM        35A    1Ø 2Ø
```

ALWGPH (Allow Graphics)

Level	Conditioning	Parameters
File	Yes	None
Record		

This keyword allows a record format to overlay any GDDM graphic images on the screen.

```
....1....+....2....+....3....+....4....+....5....+....6....+....7....+....8
A          R FORMAT1                         ALWGPH
```

ALWROL (Allow Roll)

Level	Conditioning	Parameters
Record	No	None

This keyword lets you page through data on the screen in a defined window area. Don't confuse this function with subfiles or windows. With the ALWROL keyword, all rolling is done from within the HLL program. In Cobol, you must use the WRITE ROLLING statement. In RPG, you would have to use the 5250 data-stream control codes.

```
....1....+....2....+....3....+....4....+....5....+....6....+....7....+....8
A          R FORMAT1                    ALWROL
```

ASSUME (Assume)

Level	Conditioning	Parameters
Record	No	None

This keyword prevents the current screen image from being cleared when the display file that contains the ASSUME keyword is opened.

```
....1....+....2....+....3....+....4....+....5....+....6....+....7....+....8
A          R FORMAT1                    ASSUME
```

AUTO (Auto)

Level	Conditioning	Parameters
Field	No	1) Check code

This keyword is the equivalent of the CHECK keyword for certain keyboard control functions. The CHECK keyword is recommended.

PARAMETER DEFINITION

Check code

The table below shows the valid codes for this parameter, how they map to the CHECK keyword, and their meanings:

Code	CHECK	Meaning
RA	CHECK(ER)	Auto enter
RAB	CHECK(RB)	Right-adjust blank fill
RAZ	CHECK(RZ)	Right-adjust zero fill

```
....1....+....2....+....3....+....4....+....5....+....6....+....7....+....8
A          R FORMAT1
A            FIELD1         10    B 10 21AUTO(RA)
```

BLANKS (Blanks)

Level	Conditioning	Parameters
Field	No	1) Response indicator
		2) Text (optional)

This keyword informs your HLL program that a user has entered blanks into a numeric field. The BLANKS keyword lets you determine the difference between a user-entered 0 and the field being blanked out.

PARAMETER DEFINITIONS

Response indicator
This parameter specifies the indicator to be turned on when the user enters blanks into the numeric field. Valid values are from 01 to 99.

Text
This parameter contains up to 50 characters of text to serve as documentation. You code the text within apostrophes (').

```
....1....+....2....+....3....+....4....+....5....+....6....+....7....+....8
A          R FORMAT1
A            FIELD1        7Y 0B 10 21BLANKS(44 'Field 1 is blank')
```

BLINK (Blink Cursor)

Level	Conditioning	Parameters
Record	Yes	None

This keyword causes the cursor to blink on the screen. Most workstations let the user control this feature by permitting the workstation setting to override the BLINK keyword.

```
....1....+....2....+....3....+....4....+....5....+....6....+....7....+....8
A          R FORMAT1                      BLINK
```

BLKFOLD (Blank Fold)

Level	Conditioning	Parameters
Record	Yes	None

This keyword causes an output-only field to split the text at word boundaries. The size of the field on the screen does not increase, so text may be truncated (refer also to the WRDWRAP keyword).

```
....1....+....2....+....3....+....4....+....5....+....6....+....7....+....8
A          R FORMAT1
A            FIELD1       600A  O  2  2BLKFOLD
```

CAnn (Command Attention)

Level	Conditioning	Parameters
File	Yes	1) Response indicator (optional)
Record		2) Text (optional)

This keyword activates a command key for the user. "Command attention" refers to the fact that all screen validity checking is bypassed. Generally, no screen data is returned to the program when the user presses a command attention key. The valid values for CAnn are from CA01 to CA24.

   CAnn and CFnn definitions in the same display file are mutually exclusive; for example, if you specify CA01, you cannot specify CF01.

PARAMETER DEFINITIONS

Response indicator
This optional parameter turns on an indicator when the user presses the command key. The valid values are from 01 to 99.

Text
This parameter contains up to 50 characters of text to serve as documentation. You code the text within apostrophes (').

```
....1....+....2....+....3....+....4....+....5....+....6....+....7....+....8
A                                          CA03(03 'Exit')
A          R FORMAT1                        CA12(12 'Cancel')
A   33                                      CA24
```

CFnn (Command Function)

Level	Conditioning	Parameters
File	Yes	1) Response indicator (optional)
Record		2) Text (optional)

This keyword activates a command key for the user. "Command function" refers to the fact that all screen validity checking is performed before control is returned to the HLL program. When the user presses a command function key, the system returns screen data to the program. The valid values for CFnn are from CF01 to CF24.

   CFnn and CAnn definitions within the same display file are mutually exclusive; for example, if you specify CF01, you cannot specify CA01.

PARAMETER DEFINITIONS
Response indicator
This optional parameter turns on an indicator when the command key is pressed. The valid values are from 01 to 99.

Text

The text parameter contains up to 50 characters of text to serve as documentation. You code the text within apostrophes (').

```
....1....+....2....+....3....+....4....+....5....+....6....+....7....+....8
A                                       CFØ1(Ø1 'Help')
A          R FORMAT1                     CFØ5(Ø5 'Print')
A   34                                   CF23
```

CHANGE (Change)

Level	Conditioning	Parameters
Record	No	1) Response indicator
Field		2) Text (optional)

This keyword turns on the specified indicator whenever the user changes the content of a field. When you specify the keyword at the record-format level, the indicator is turned on when any field for that format is changed. A field is considered changed if the user types any data into a field, even if the data is the same as the original field content.

PARAMETER DEFINITIONS

Response indicator

This parameter specifies the indicator to be turned on when the user changes the contents of a field. The parameter is a number from 01 to 99.

Text

The text parameter contains up to 50 characters of text to serve as documentation. You code the text within apostrophes (').

```
....1....+....2....+....3....+....4....+....5....+....6....+....7....+....8
A          R FORMAT1
A            FIELD1        10   B 10 21CHANGE(41 'Field 1 changed')
```

CHCACCEL (Choice Accelerator Text)

Level	Conditioning	Parameters
Field	No	1) Choice number
		2) Accelerator text

This keyword lets you assign text to a choice option that normally corresponds to some type of function key. This option only assigns the text; it does not activate the command key. You must still specify the CAnn or CFnn.

You can specify this keyword only for fields using the SNGCHCFLD keyword within a pull-down menu (see the discussion about the PULLDOWN keyword).

Parameter Definitions

Choice number

This parameter is a number from 01 to 99 that corresponds to the choice option being defined (see the CHOICE keyword).

Accelerator text

This parameter defines the text to be displayed. You can either hard-code the text within apostrophes or use a program-to-system field to let your HLL program send the text to the screen. If you use a program-to-system field, the field must be defined within the same record format, have a data type of A, and have a usage of P.

```
....1....+....2....+....3....+....4....+....5....+....6....+....7....+....8
A            R FORMAT1                 CF04
A                                      CF06
A                                      PULLDOWN
A              FIELD1        2Y 0B  1  2SNGCHCFLD
A                                      CHOICE(1 'Update')
A                                      CHOICE(2 'Add')
A                                      CHOICE(3 'Delete')
A                                      CHCACCEL(1 'F4')
A                                      CHCACCEL(2 &F6)
A              F6           2A  P
```

CHCAVAIL (Choice Color/Attribute when Available)

Level	Conditioning	Parameters
Field	Yes	1) Color (optional)
		2) Display attribute (optional)
		NOTE: At least one of the parameters must be provided.

This keyword lets you indicate the color or display attribute of the choice text when that choice is valid for the user. You control whether a choice is valid by means of the CHCCTL keyword. This keyword is valid only when the field also uses either the PSHBTNCHC, CHOICE, or MNUBARCHC keyword.

Parameter Definitions

Color

This parameter specifies the color to be used for the choice text. The parameter has two elements: *COLOR and one of the following color identifiers:

- (*COLOR GRN)   Green
- (*COLOR RED)   Red
- (*COLOR BLU)   Blue
- (*COLOR WHT)   White

- (*COLOR TRQ)   Turquoise
- (*COLOR YLW)   Yellow
- (*COLOR PNK)   Pink

The default color is green.

Display attribute

This parameter specifies the display attribute to be used for the choice text. The parameter has two elements: *DSPATR and one of the following display attributes:

- (*DSPATR BL)   Blink
- (*DSPATR CS)   Column Separator
- (*DSPATR HI)   High Intensity
- (*DSPATR ND)   Non-Display
- (*DSPATR RI)   Reverse Image
- (*DSPATR UL)   Underline

The default display attribute is HI for menu bars and normal video for selection fields.

You can specify more than one display attribute after the *DSPATR code; for example, (*DSPATR HI RI).

```
....1....+....2....+....3....+....4....+....5....+....6....+....7....+....8
A          R FORMAT1
A                                      PULLDOWN
A            FIELD1        2Y 0B  1  2SNGCHCFLD
A                                      CHOICE(1 'Update')
A                                      CHOICE(2 'Add')
A                                      CHOICE(3 'Delete')
A                                      CHCCTL(1 &CHC1)
A                                      CHCCTL(2 &CHC2)
A                                      CHCAVAIL((*DSPATR HI))
A            CHC1          1Y 0H
A            CHC2          1Y 0H
```

CHCCTL (Choice Control)

Level	Conditioning	Parameters
Field	No	1) Choice number
		2) Control field
		3) Message ID (optional)
		4) Message file (optional)

This keyword serves two functions. First, on output from your HLL program, you can set the availability of a choice for a choice field. Then, on input from the screen, your HLL program can determine which choice the user selected.

PARAMETER DEFINITIONS

Choice number

This parameter is the number of the choice you wish to control. The parameter is a number from 1 to 99.

Control field

This parameter is the name of a field that can communicate with your HLL program. You must define this field within the same record format, and the field must have a data type of Y, be one digit long with zero decimal positions, and have a usage of H.

The following table shows the values you can use with the control field:

Value	Meaning on Output	Meaning on Input
0	Available	Not selected by user
1	Set as default	Selected by user
2	Unavailable (user cannot place cursor on this choice unless help has been defined for this choice number)	
3	Unavailable (user can place cursor on choice)	
4	Unavailable (user cannot place cursor on this choice)	

Message ID

This optional parameter lets you specify the message to be displayed when the user selects a choice that is not available. You can specify this value within the DDS, or you can use a variable field. If you use a variable field, you must define the field within the same record format and the field must have a data type of A, be seven characters long, and have a usage of P.

Message file

This optional parameter is required when you specify a message ID. The message file parameter specifies the name of the message file in which the message ID is located. You can qualify the file name with the name of the library if you wish. You can hard-code the message file name or use a variable field. If you use a variable field for the message file name or the library name, you must define the field within the same record format and it must have a data type of A, be 10 characters long, and have a usage of P.

```
....1....+....2....+....3....+....4....+....5....+....6....+....7....+....8
A          R FORMAT1
A                                         PULLDOWN
A            FIELD1        2Y 0B   1  2SNGCHCFLD
A                                         CHOICE(1 'Update')
A                                         CHOICE(2 'Add')
A                                         CHOICE(3 'Delete')
A                                         CHCCTL(1 &CHC1)
A                                         CHCCTL(2 &CHC2 USR0001 USERMSGF)
A                                         CHCCTL(3 &CHC3 &MSGID &MSGL/&MSGF)
A            CHC1          1Y 0H
A            CHC2          1Y 0H
A            CHC3          1Y 0H
A            MSGID         7A   P
A            MSGL         10A   P
A            MSGF         10A   P
```

CHCSLT (Choice Color/Attribute when Selected)

Level	Conditioning	Parameters
Field	Yes	1) Color (optional)
		2) Display attribute (optional)
		NOTE: One parameter must be specified.

This keyword lets you indicate the color or display attribute of the choice text when the user selects that choice. CHCSLT is valid only when the field also contains either the CHOICE or the MNUBARCHC keyword.

PARAMETER DEFINITIONS

Color

This parameter specifies the color to be used for the choice text. The parameter has two elements: *COLOR and one of the following color identifiers:

- (*COLOR GRN)   Green
- (*COLOR RED)   Red
- (*COLOR BLU)   Blue
- (*COLOR WHT)   White
- (*COLOR TRQ)   Turquoise
- (*COLOR YLW)   Yellow
- (*COLOR PNK)   Pink

The default color is white.

Display attribute

This parameter specifies the display attribute to be used for the choice text. The parameter has two elements: *DSPATR and one of the following display attributes:

- (*DSPATR BL) Blink
- (*DSPATR CS) Column Separator
- (*DSPATR HI) High Intensity
- (*DSPATR ND) Nondisplay
- (*DSPATR RI) Reverse Image
- (*DSPATR UL) Underline

The default display attribute is normal video for a menu bar and HI for selections in a pull-down menu.

You can specify more than one display attribute after the *DSPATR code; for example, (*DSPATR HI RI).

```
....1....+....2....+....3....+....4....+....5....+....6....+....7....+....8
A            R FORMAT1
A                                          PULLDOWN
A              FIELD1        2Y 0B  1 2SNGCHCFLD
A                                          CHOICE(1 'Update')
A                                          CHOICE(2 'Add')
A                                          CHOICE(3 'Delete')
A                                          CHCCTL(1 &CHC1)
A                                          CHCCTL(2 &CHC2)
A                                          CHCSLT((*DSPATR HI))
A              CHC1          1Y 0H
A              CHC2          1Y 0H
```

CHCUNAVAIL (Choice Color/Attribute when Unavailable)

Level	Conditioning	Parameters
Field	Yes	1) Color (optional)
		2) Display attribute (optional)
		NOTE: At least one of the parameters must be provided.

This keyword lets you indicate the color or display attribute of the choice text when the choice is not valid for the user. You control whether a choice is valid by means of the CHCCTL keyword. CHCUNAVAIL is valid only when the field also includes either the PSHBTNCHC or the CHOICE keyword.

PARAMETER DEFINITIONS

Color
This parameter specifies the color to be used for the choice text. The parameter has two elements: *COLOR and one of the following color identifiers:

- (*COLOR GRN)   Green
- (*COLOR RED)   Red
- (*COLOR BLU)   Blue
- (*COLOR WHT)   White
- (*COLOR TRQ)   Turquoise
- (*COLOR YLW)   Yellow
- (*COLOR PNK)   Pink

The default color is blue.

Display attribute

This parameter specifies which display attribute is to be used for the choice text. The parameter has two elements: *DSPATR and one of the following display attributes:

- (*DSPATR BL)   Blink
- (*DSPATR CS)   Column separator
- (*DSPATR HI)   High intensity
- (*DSPATR ND)   Nondisplay
- (*DSPATR RI)   Reverse image
- (*DSPATR UL)   Underline

The default display attribute is normal video.

You can specify more than one display attribute after the *DSPATR code; for example, (*DSPATR HI RI).

```
....1....+....2....+....3....+....4....+....5....+....6....+....7....+....8
A          R FORMAT1
A            FIELD1        2Y 0B  1  2SNGCHCFLD
A                                    CHOICE(1 'Update')
A                                    CHOICE(2 'Add')
A                                    CHOICE(3 'Delete')
A                                    CHCCTL(1 &CHC1)
A                                    CHCCTL(2 &CHC2)
A                                    CHCUNAVAIL((*COLOR PNK))
A            CHC1          1Y 0H
A            CHC2          1Y 0H
```

CHECK (Check)

Level	Conditioning	Parameters
Field	No	1) Check code

This keyword specifies validity checking for a field. You can also use CHECK to control special keyboard controls and cursor movements.

You can specify this keyword at the file or record-format level only when CHECK(AB) is used. Also, you can use conditioning indicators only for CHECK(ER) and CHECK(ME).

PARAMETER DEFINITION

Check code

The table below shows the valid codes for validity checking.

Code	Meaning
AB	Allow blanks
ME	Mandatory entry
MF	Mandatory fill
M10	Modulus 10 self-check
M10F	Modulus 10 self-check
M11	Modulus 11 self-check
M11F	Modulus 11 self-check
VN	Valid name
VNE	Valid name extended

You can specify more than one validity checking code in the same CHECK keyword.

Following are the valid codes for controlling certain data-entry aspects:

Code	Meaning
ER	End of record
FE	Field exit required
LC	Lowercase entry allowed
RB	Right-adjust, blank fill
RZ	Right-adjust, zero fill

You can specify more than one keyboard control code in a single CHECK keyword.

The following codes are available to control cursor movement. These values work only for terminals that support right-to-left movement.

Code	Meaning
RL	Right to left within a field
RLTB	Right to left, top to bottom, from field to field

```
....1....+....2....+....3....+....4....+....5....+....6....+....7....+....8
A          R FORMAT1
A            CUSNBR        7S 0B 10 10CHECK(M10)
A            CUSNAM       35A  B 10 20CHECK(ME)
```

CHGINPDFT (Change Input Default)

Level	Conditioning	Parameters
File	No	1) Input default
Record		
Field		

This keyword changes the default attributes for an input-capable field.

PARAMETER DEFINITION

Input default

The table below shows the valid codes for this parameter and their meanings.

Code	Meaning
Blank	Remove underline
BL	Blink field
CS	Column separators
HI	Highlight field
RI	Reverse-image field
UL	Underline field
FE	Field exit required
LC	Lowercase entry allowed
ME	Mandatory entry
MF	Mandatory fill

```
....1....+....2....+....3....+....4....+....5....+....6....+....7....+....8
A          R FORMAT1                    CHGINPDFT
A            CUSNBR        7S ØB 1Ø 1Ø
A            CUSNAM       35A  B 1Ø 2ØCHGINPDFT(CS)
```

CHKMSGID (Check Message Identifier)

Level	Conditioning	Parameters
Field	No	1) Message ID
		2) Message file
		3) Message data (optional)

This keyword overrides the message displayed when the user enters data that violates the validity-checking keyword for the field.

PARAMETER DEFINITIONS

Message ID

This parameter is the seven-character message ID that contains the text to be displayed.

Message file
This parameter is the name of the file that contains the message ID. You can qualify the file name with the name of the library if you wish.

Message data
This optional parameter lets you send data to the message ID. This field name must be defined within the same record format and must have a data type of A and a usage of P.

```
....1....+....2....+....3....+....4....+....5....+....6....+....7....+....8
A          R FORMAT1
A            CUSNBR        7S 0B 10 10CHECK(M10)
A                                   CHKMSGID(USR0002 USERMSGF)
A            CUSNAM       35A  B 10 20CHECK(ME)
A                                   CHKMSGID(USR0003 USERMSGF &DATA)
A            DATA         10A  P
```

CHOICE (Choice)

Level	Conditioning	Parameters
Field	No	1) Choice number
		2) Choice text
		3) Spacing (optional)

This keyword specifies the choices available for a choice selection field. You must use this keyword in connection with either the SNGCHCFLD or the MLTCHCFLD keyword. You code one CHOICE keyword for each choice available for a field.

PARAMETER DEFINITIONS

Choice number
This parameter is a number from 01 to 99. Each choice must have a unique number assigned.

Choice text
This parameter is the text to be shown for the choice. You can either hard-code the text in the DDS or use a variable field. If you use a variable field, that field must be defined in the same record format and must have a data type of A and a usage of P.

   You can also specify a mneumonic for the choice within the text by placing a > sign before the character that will act as the mneumonic. That character will appear on the screen underlined.

Spacing

This optional parameter lets you insert a blank line before the specified choice. The only valid value is *SPACEB.

```
....1....+....2....+....3....+....4....+....5....+....6....+....7....+....8
A          R FORMAT1
A            FIELD1         2Y 0B  1  2SNGCHCFLD
A                                     CHOICE(1 '>Update')
A                                     CHOICE(2 '>Add')
A                                     CHOICE(3 '>Delete')
A                                     CHIOCE(5 &TEXT *SPACEB)
A            TEXT          10A  P
```

CHRID (Character Identifier)

Level	Conditioning	Parameters
Field	No	None

This keyword indicates that a character set other than the default can be used for the field.

```
....1....+....2....+....3....+....4....+....5....+....6....+....7....+....8
A          R FORMAT1
A            CUSNAM        35A     10 20CHRID
```

CLEAR (Clear)

Level	Conditioning	Parameters
File	Yes	1) Response indicator (optional)
Record		2) Text (optional)

This keyword informs your HLL program when the user has pressed the Clear key. The Clear key acts like a command attention key — that is, it indicates that no screen validity checking will be performed.

PARAMETER DEFINITIONS

Response indicator

This optional parameter specifies the indicator to be turned on when the user presses Clear. The valid values are 01 to 99.

Text

The text parameter contains up to 50 characters of text to serve as documentation for this keyword. You code the text within apostrophes (').

```
....1....+....2....+....3....+....4....+....5....+....6....+....7....+....8
A          R FORMAT1
A                                     CLEAR(29 'Clear requested')
```

CLRL (Clear Line)

Level	Conditioning	Parameters
Record	No	1) Number of lines

This keyword clears a specific number of lines on the screen before the record format is written to the screen.

PARAMETER DEFINITION

Number of lines

Four values are valid for this parameter:

- nn — a number from 01 to 27 that indicates the number of lines to clear, starting with the first line defined in the record format. The specified number cannot exceed the size of the display file.

- *END — indicates that the lines from the first line defined in the record format to the end of the screen are to be cleared.

- *ALL — indicates that all lines on the screen are to be cleared.

- *NO — indicates that no lines are to be cleared on the screen before writing the record format. This is the most common use of this keyword.

```
....1....+....2....+....3....+....4....+....5....+....6....+....7....+....8
A          R FORMAT1
A                                             CLRL(*NO)
A            CUSNBR        7S 0  10 10
A            CUSNAM       35A     10 20
```

CMP (Comparison)

Level	Conditioning	Parameters
Field	No	1) Compare code
		2) Value

This keyword is the same as the COMP keyword, but COMP is preferred.

PARAMETER DEFINITIONS

Compare code

The valid comparison codes for this parameter are

Code	Meaning
EQ	Equal
NE	Not equal
LT	Less than
NL	Not less than
GT	Greater than
NG	Not greater than
LE	Less than or equal to
GE	Greater than or equal to

Value

This parameter is the value that the field will be compared against.

```
....1....+....2....+....3....+....4....+....5....+....6....+....7....+....8
A          R FORMAT1
A            CUSNBR       7S 0B 10 10CMP(GT 0)
A            CUSNAM      35A  B 10 20CMP(NE ' ')
```

CNTFLD (Continued Entry Field)

Level	Conditioning	Parameters
Field	No	1) Width

This keyword breaks a large input field into small segments on the screen. The field is treated just as if it had not been broken into segments.

PARAMETER DEFINITION

Width

This parameter is a number that indicates the size of each segment on the screen. The last line on the screen may be smaller than the other lines because of the size of the field.

```
....1....+....2....+....3....+....4....+....5....+....6....+....7....+....8
A          R FORMAT1
A            FIELD       500A  B 10 10CNTFLD(60)
```

COLOR (Color)

Level	Conditioning	Parameters
Field	Yes	1) Color

This keyword lets you display a field in color on workstations that support color. The COLOR keyword is ignored on noncolor terminals.

PARAMETER DEFINITION

Color

This parameter is the value indicating the color you wish to display. Following
are the valid codes and their meanings for this parameter:

Color	Meaning
BLU	Blue
GRN	Green
PNK	Pink
RED	Red
TRQ	Turquoise
WHT	White
YLW	Yellow

```
....1....+....2....+....3....+....4....+....5....+....6....+....7....+....8
A              R FORMAT1
A                CUSNBR        7S 0   10 10COLOR(GRN)
A                CUSNAM       35A     10 20
A    40                                  COLOR(RED)
```

COMP (Comparison)

Level	Conditioning	Parameters
Field	No	1) Compare code
		2) Value

This keyword compares the field on the screen with the specified value. If the
comparison is false, the user is notified of the error.

PARAMETER DEFINITIONS

Compare code

The table below shows the valid comparison codes for this parameter.

Code	Meaning
EQ	Equal
NE	Not equal
LT	Less than
NL	Not less than
GT	Greater than
NG	Not greater than
LE	Less than or equal to
GE	Greater than or equal to

Value

This parameter contains the value against which the field is to be compared.

```
....1....+....2....+....3....+....4....+....5....+....6....+....7....+....8
A           R FORMAT1
A             CUSNBR          7S 0B 10 10COMP(GT 0)
A             CUSNAM         35A  B 10 20COMP(NE ' ')
```

CSRINPONLY (Cursor Movement to Input Positions Only)

Level	Conditioning	Parameters
File	Yes	None
Record		

This keyword restricts movement of the cursor on screen to input-capable fields only. CSRINPONLY affects the use of the arrow keys.

```
....1....+....2....+....3....+....4....+....5....+....6....+....7....+....8
A           R FORMAT1
A                                             CSRINPONLY
A             CUSNBR          7S 00 10 10
A             CUSNAM         35A  B 10 20
```

CSRLOC (Cursor Location)

Level	Conditioning	Parameters
Record	Yes	1) Line number
		2) Column

This keyword positions the cursor to a specific location on the screen when the record format is written. CSRLOC overrides all other cursor-positioning keywords.

PARAMETER DEFINITIONS

Line number

This parameter contains the number of the line to which the cursor is to be positioned. This field is be defined within the same record format, has a data type of S, is three digits long with zero decimal positions, and has a usage of H.

Column

This parameter contains the number of the column to which the cursor is to be positioned. This field is defined within the same record format, has a data type of S, is three digits long with zero decimal positions, and has a usage of H.

```
....1....+....2....+....3....+....4....+....5....+....6....+....7....+....8
A           R FORMAT1
A                                             CSRLOC(ROW COL)
A             CUSNBR          7S 0B 10 10
A             CUSNAM         35A  B 10 20
A             ROW             3S 0H
A             COL             3S 0H
```

DATE (Date)

Level	Conditioning	Parameters
Field	No	1) Date to display (optional)
		2) Format of date (optional)

This keyword displays a date on the screen. You can display either the job or system date.

PARAMETER DEFINITIONS

Date to display
This parameter specifies which date to display. *JOB indicates that the job date is to be displayed; *JOB is the default. *SYS displays the system date.

Format of date
This parameter specifies how the date is displayed on the screen. A value of *Y displays a two-digit year, while *YY displays a four-digit year. *Y is the default.

```
....1....+....2....+....3....+....4....+....5....+....6....+....7....+....8
A              R FORMAT1
A                                      1   2DATE

A              R FORMAT2
A                                      1   2DATE(*YY)

A              R FORMAT3
A                                      1   2DATE(*SYS *Y)
```

DATFMT (Date Format)

Level	Conditioning	Parameters
Field	No	1) Date format

This keyword lets you specify the format of a date field. This keyword can be specified only on a field with a data type of L.

PARAMETER DEFINITION

Date format
This parameter defines how the date will appear on the screen. The following table shows the valid values for this parameter.

Date Format	Meaning	Format
*JOB	Job default	—
*YMD	Year/month/day	yy/mm/dd
*MDY	Month/day/year	mm/dd/yy
*DMY	Day/month/year	dd/mm/yy
*JUL	Julian	yy/ddd
*ISO	International Standards Organization	yyyy-mm-dd
*USA	USA standard	mm/dd/yyyy
*EUR	European standard	dd.mm.yyyy
*JIS	Japanese industrial standard	yyyy-mm-dd

```
....1....+....2....+....3....+....4....+....5....+....6....+....7....+....8
A          R FORMAT1
A            FIELD1         L    10 10DATFMT(*ISO)
```

DATSEP (Date Separator)

Level	Conditioning	Parameters
Field	No	1) Date separator

This keyword defines the separator to be used for a date field (data type L). If the date field is defined as *ISO, *USA, *EUR, or *JIS, you cannot specify this keyword.

PARAMETER DEFINITION

Date separator

This parameter is either an explicit value defined within apostrophes (') or a value of *JOB. The valid values are slash (/), dash (-), period (.), comma (,), and blank ( ). *JOB indicates you are to use the job's default separator.

```
....1....+....2....+....3....+....4....+....5....+....6....+....7....+....8
A          R FORMAT1
A            FIELD1         L    10 10DATFMT(*YMD)
A                                  DATSEP('.')
```

DFT (Default)

Level	Conditioning	Parameters
Field	No	1) Value

This keyword lets you specify a default display value. DFT is used mainly for input-only fields. When DFT is used with output or input/output fields, you must also use the PUTOVR and OVRDTA keywords.

PARAMETER DEFINITION

Value

This parameter is the default value you wish to show on the screen. It must be enclosed within single quotes (').

```
....1....+....2....+....3....+....4....+....5....+....6....+....7....+....8
A              R FORMAT1
A                FIELD1        1A  I 10 10DFT('A')
```

DFTVAL (Default Value)

Level	Conditioning	Parameters
Field	Yes	1) Value

This keyword lets you specify a default display value for output and input/output-only fields.

PARAMETER DEFINITION

Value

This parameter is the default value you wish to show on the screen. It must be enclosed within apostrophes (').

```
....1....+....2....+....3....+....4....+....5....+....6....+....7....+....8
A              R FORMAT1
A                FIELD1        1A  B 10 10DFT('A')
```

DLTCHK (Delete Check)

Level	Conditioning	Parameters
Record	Yes	None

This keyword removes any validity-checking keywords that would normally be copied from a referenced field.

```
....1....+....2....+....3....+....4....+....5....+....6....+....7....+....8
A              R FORMAT1
A                CUSNBR     R        10 10REFFLD(CUST# REFFILE)
A                                       DLTCHK
```

DLTEDT (Delete Edit)

Level	Conditioning	Parameters
Field	No	None

This keyword removes EDTCDE and EDTWRD definitions that would normally be copied from a referenced field.

```
....1....+....2....+....3....+....4....+....5....+....6....+....7....+....8
A            R FORMAT1
A              CUSNBR       R          10 10REFFLD(CUST# REFFILE)
A                                         DLTEDT
```

DSPATR (Display Attribute)

Level	Conditioning	Parameters
Field	Yes	1) Attribute

This keyword changes the display attribute of a field on the screen.

PARAMETER DEFINITION

Attribute

This parameter is a code that indicates the attribute to be used. The table below shows the valid codes.

Code	Meaning
BL	Blink field
CS	Column separator
HI	Highlight field
ND	Nondisplay field
PC	Position cursor to field
RI	Reverse image field
UL	Underline field

In addition to the codes listed above, the following codes are available for input-capable fields:

Code	Meaning
MDT	Set modified data tag
OID	Allow magnetic strip reader for field
PR	Protect input field from changes
SP	Allow light pen for field selection

You can specify more than one attribute per DSPATR keyword.

You can also use a variable field name to specify the display attribute from your HLL program. This field must be defined within the same record format, have a data type of A, be one character long, and have a usage of P. You can specify only one field name per DSPATR keyword.

The following table shows the valid codes that can be sent via a field name.

Hex value	Corresponding DSPATR value	Hex value	Corresponding DSPATR value
20	Default	A0	Default, PR
21	RI	A1	RI PR
22	HI	A2	HI PR
23	RI HI	A3	RI HI PR
24	UL	A4	UL PR
25	UL RI	A5	UL RI PR
26	UL HI	A6	UL HI PR
27	ND	A7	ND PR
28	BL	A8	BL PR
29	BL RI	A9	BL RI PR
2A	BL HI	AA	BL HI PR
2B	BL RI HI	AB	BL RI HI PR
2C	BL UL	AC	BL UL PR
2D	BL UL RI	AD	BL UL RI PR
2E	BL UL HI	AE	BL UL HI PR
2F	ND	AF	ND PR
30	Default, CS	B0	Default, CS PR
31	CS RI	B1	CS RI PR
32	CS HI	B2	CS HI PR
33	CS RI HI	B3	CS RI HI PR
34	CS UL	B4	CS UL PR
35	CS UL RI	B5	CS UL RI PR
36	CS UL HI	B6	CS UL HI PR
37	ND	B7	ND PR
38	CS BL	B8	CS BL PR
39	CS BL RI	B9	CS BL RI PR
3A	CS BL HI	BA	CS BL HI PR
3B	CS BL RI HI	BB	CS BL RI HI PR
3C	CS BL UL	BC	CS BL UL PR
3D	CS BL UL RI	BD	CS BL UL RI PR
3E	CS BL UL HI	BE	CS BL UL HI PR
3F	ND	BF	ND PR

```
....1....+....2....+....3....+....4....+....5....+....6....+....7....+....8

A          R FORMAT1
A            CUSNBR        7S 0   10 10DSPATR(HI UL)
A            CUSNAM        35A    10 20DSPATR(&ATTRIB)
A            ATTRIB        1A  P
```

DSPMOD (Display Mode)

Level	Conditioning	Parameters
Record	Yes	1) Condition name

This keyword sets the display size to be used when the record format is sent to the screen. You use DSPMOD in connection with the DSPSIZ keyword.

PARAMETER DEFINITION

Condition name

This parameter is the name of the screen size to be used. This name corresponds to that set by the DSPSIZ keyword.

```
....1....+....2....+....3....+....4....+....5....+....6....+....7....+....8
A
A                                          DSPSIZ(*DS3 *DS4)
A        R FORMAT1
A    40                                     DSPMOD(*DS4)
```

DSPRL (Display Right to Left)

Level	Conditioning	Parameters
File	No	None

This keyword indicates that all fields sent to the screen are to be shown in right-to-left order. DSPRL is valid only for workstations that have bidirectional support.

```
....1....+....2....+....3....+....4....+....5....+....6....+....7....+....8
A
A                                          DSPRL
A        R FORMAT1
A                        10 10'txet elpmaS'
```

DSPSIZ (Display Size)

Level	Conditioning	Parameters
File	No	1) Primary size
		2) Secondary size (optional)

This keyword defines on which screen sizes the display file can be shown. You use DSPSIZ mainly to display data on wide-screen terminals.

PARAMETER DEFINITIONS

Primary size

This parameter indicates which screen size is to be used as the default. You can use one of two methods to specify the screen size.

The first method is to use a special condition name: *DS3 or *DS4. *DS3 indicates a screen size of 24 x 80; *DS4 a screen size of 27 x 132.

Alternatively, you can explicitly specify the screen size by entering either 24 80 or 27 132. When you specify the size of the screen explicitly, you can optionally specify a user-defined condition name. The condition name can be from 2 to 8 characters long and must start with an asterisk (*). You can also use the special values of *DS3 and *DS4 for the condition name.

Secondary size

This optional parameter indicates the secondary screen size that the display file can use. The specifications for this parameter are the same as for the primary size parameter.

NOTE: You can use conditioning names in columns 7 through 16 to control the location of a field on the screen. Conditioning names specify an alternate location; they are never used on the actual field line. Most keywords do not allow the use of a conditioning name in columns 7 through 16.

```
....1....+....2....+....3....+....4....+....5....+....6....+....7....+....8
A                                    DSPSIZ(*DS3)
A          R FORMAT1

....1....+....2....+....3....+....4....+....5....+....6....+....7....+....8
A                                    DSPSIZ(27 132 24 80)
A          R FORMAT1
A            CUSNBR        7S 0    10 90
A            CUSNAM        35A     11 90

....1....+....2....+....3....+....4....+....5....+....6....+....7....+....8
A                                    DSPSIZ(24 80 *DS3 27 132 *LARGE)
A          R FORMAT1
A            CUSNBR        7S 0    10 10
A  *LARGE                          10 90
A            CUSNAM        35A     10 20
```

DUP (Duplication)

Level	Conditioning	Parameters
Field	Yes	1) Response indicator (optional)
		2) Text (optional)

This keyword specifies that the DUP key is allowed for the field. It's important to note that the AS/400 does not duplicate any data (duplication is the job of your HLL program).

For character fields, the system places X'1C' in the field from the cursor location to the end of the field to indicate duplication is requested.

For numeric fields, the system uses a value X 'F0' to indicate duplication when a response indicator is specified. Otherwise, X'1C' is used.

PARAMETER DEFINITIONS

Response indicator

This optional parameter specifies the indicator that is to be turned on when the user presses the Dup key. The valid values are 01 to 99.

Text

The text parameter contains up to 50 characters of text to serve as documentation for the keyword. You code the text within apostrophes (').

```
....1....+....2....+....3....+....4....+....5....+....6....+....7....+....8
A          R FORMAT1
A            CUSNBR       7S 0B 10 10
A            CUSNAM      35A  B 10 20DUP(31 'Dup customer name')
```

EDTCDE (Edit Code)

Level	Conditioning	Parameters
Field	No	1) Edit code
		2) Floating symbol (optional)

This keyword defines the format a numeric field will have when displayed on the screen. Each edit code has a different effect on how the data is displayed.

PARAMETER DEFINITIONS

Edit code

This parameter is a valid AS/400 edit code. The following table shows the valid codes and their effect on the number when it is displayed.

Code	Commas Printed	Decimal Points Printed	Negative Sign Shown	Zero Value
1	Yes	Yes	No Sign	0 printed
2	Yes	Yes	No Sign	Blanks
3	No	Yes	No Sign	0 printed
4	No	Yes	No Sign	Blanks
A	Yes	Yes	CR	0 printed
B	Yes	Yes	CR	Blanks
C	No	Yes	CR	0 printed
D	No	Yes	CR	Blanks
J	Yes	Yes	- (Minus)	0 printed
K	Yes	Yes	- (Minus)	Blanks
L	No	Yes	- (Minus)	0 printed
M	No	Yes	- (Minus)	Blanks
N	Yes	Yes	- (Minus)	0 printed
O	Yes	Yes	- (Minus)	Blanks

Code	Commas Printed	Decimal Points Printed	Negative Sign Shown	Zero Value
P	No	Yes	- (Minus)	0 printed
Q	No	Yes	- (Minus)	Blanks
W	No	No	Blank	0/000
Y	No	No	Blank	0/00/00
Z	No	No	Blank	Blanks

Edit codes J-M place the minus sign after the number. Edit codes N-Q place the minus sign before the number.

The W edit code suppresses the leftmost digit of five-digit date fields and the three leftmost digits of date fields that are six to eight digits long. The W edit code places a slash (/) between the year, month, and day data in the date field.

Edit code Y is similar to the W edit code, but is used with non-date fields that contain date values.

Floating symbol

This optional parameter is either an asterisk (*) or any other character you choose to act as a floating currency symbol. An asterisk indicates that the numeric field is to have all leading zeros replaced by asterisks. The floating character appears to the left of the most significant digit.

```
....1....+....2....+....3....+....4....+....5....+....6....+....7....+....8
A           R FORMAT1
A             CUSNBR      7P 0   10 10EDTCDE(4)
A             CUSNAM     35A     10 25
A             ORDNBR      7P 0   11 10EDTCDE(4)
A             SLSAMT      9P 2   11 45EDTCDE(L)
```

EDTMSK (Edit Mask)

Level	Conditioning	Parameters
Field	No	1) Edit mask

This keyword defines an input mask to protect areas in a numeric field coded with the EDTCDE or EDTWRD keyword (for example, preventing the user from entering data over the date separators for a field with EDTCDE(Y) specified).

PARAMETER DEFINITION

Edit mask

This parameter, a character string within apostrophes, defines the edit mask. You code an ampersand (&) for each position of the numeric field to be protected. The length of the mask must not exceed the total displayed length of the field.

```
....1....+....2....+....3....+....4....+....5....+....6....+....7....+....8
A          R FORMAT1
A            STRDTE         6Y ØB 10 1ØEDTCDE(Y)
A                                    EDTMSK('  &  &  ')
A            SSN#           9Y ØB 10 2ØEDTWRD('   -  -   ')
A                                    EDTMSK('  &  &   ')
```

EDTWRD (Edit Word)

Level	Conditioning	Parameters
Field	No	1) Edit word

This keyword creates a special edit description for a numeric field when none of the AS/400 edit codes provides the formatting you need.

PARAMETER DEFINITION

Edit word

This parameter is a valid AS/400 edit-word character string.

```
....1....+....2....+....3....+....4....+....5....+....6....+....7....+....8
A          R FORMAT1
A            EMP#           7P 0   10 10
A            EMPNAM        35A     10 25
A            SSN            9P 0   11 1ØEDTWRD('   -  -   ')
```

ENTFLDATR (Entry Field Attribute)

Level	Conditioning	Parameters
File	Yes	1) Color (optional)
Record		2) Display attribute (optional)
Field		3) Cursor visible (optional)

This keyword specifies the color or display attribute of a field when the cursor is moved into that field.

PARAMETER DEFINITIONS

Color

This parameter specifies which color is to be used when the cursor is moved into the field. The parameter has two elements: *COLOR and one of the following color identifiers:

- (*COLOR GRN)   Green
- (*COLOR RED)   Red
- (*COLOR BLU)   Blue
- (*COLOR WHT)   White

- (*COLOR TRQ)   Turquoise
- (*COLOR YLW)   Yellow
- (*COLOR PNK)   Pink

The default color is white.

Display attribute

This parameter specifies which display attribute is to be used when the cursor is moved into the field. The parameter has two elements: *DSPATR and one of the following display attributes:

- (*DSPATR BL)   Blink
- (*DSPATR CS)   Column Separator
- (*DSPATR HI)   High Intensity
- (*DSPATR ND)   Nondisplay
- (*DSPATR RI)   Reverse Image
- (*DSPATR UL)   Underline

You can specify more than one display attribute after the *DSPATR code; for example, (*DSPATR HI RI).

If no display attribute is specified, the default is HI.

Cursor visible

This optional parameter specifies whether the cursor is visible when it is moved into the field. The valid values are *CURSOR, indicating the cursor is visible, and *NOCURSOR, indicating the cursor is not visible. *NOCURSOR is valid only when the field has a data type of I. The default is *CURSOR.

```
....1....+....2....+....3....+....4....+....5....+....6....+....7....+....8
A            R FORMAT1
A              CUSNBR       7S  0B 10 10ENTFLDATR((*COLOR PINK))
A              CUSNAM      35A   B 10 20ENTFLDATR((*DSPATR RI))
```

ERASE (Erase)

Level	Conditioning	Parameters
Record	Yes	1) Record name

This keyword specifies that the record format names identified in the keyword are to be removed from the screen before the record format is sent to the screen. ERASE is used in connection with the OVERLAY keyword.

PARAMETER DEFINITION

Record name

This parameter is the name of a record format that is to be removed from the screen. You can specify up to 20 record formats within this keyword.

```
....1....+....2....+....3....+....4....+....5....+....6....+....7....+....8
A              R FORMAT1
A              R FORMAT2                        ERASE(FORMAT1)
A                                               OVERLAY
A                CUSNBR          7S 0   10 10
A                CUSNAM         35A      10 20
```

ERASEINP (Erase Input)

Level	Conditioning	Parameters
Record	Yes	1) Modified tag option (optional)

This keyword erases the contents of unprotected input-capable fields that are already on the screen when the record format is sent to the screen. Input-capable fields containing the ERASEINP keyword are not cleared. Only those fields already on the screen are cleared.

ERASEINP is used in connection with the OVERLAY keyword.

PARAMETER DEFINITION

Modified tag option

This optional parameter indicates which input-capable fields are to be cleared. The valid values are *MDTON and *ALL. *MDTON clears only input fields that have been modified by the user. *ALL clears all input-capable fields. The default is *MDTON.

```
....1....+....2....+....3....+....4....+....5....+....6....+....7....+....8
A              R FORMAT1
A                FIELD1         10A  B  1 10
A              R FORMAT2
A                                               OVERLAY
A   40                                          ERASEINP(*ALL)
A                CUSNBR          7S 0B 10 10
A                CUSNAM         35A  B 10 20
```

ERRMSG (Error Message)

Level	Conditioning	Parameters
Field	Yes	1) Message text
		2) Response indicator (optional)

This keyword displays an error message for a specific field.

PARAMETER DEFINITIONS

Message text

This parameter is the error message to be displayed. The amount of text can be equivalent to the size of the screen. The text is entered within apostrophes (').

Response indicator

This optional parameter turns a specific indicator off when control is returned to your HLL program. The specified indicator is normally the same one specified in the conditioning columns.

```
....1....+....2....+....3....+....4....+....5....+....6....+....7....+....8
A            R FORMAT1
A              CUSNBR        7S 0B 10 10
A   70                                   ERRMSG('Invalid customer #')
A              CUSNAM       35A  B 10 20
A   71                                   ERRMSG('Name cannot be blank' 71)
```

ERRMSGID (Error Message Identifier)

Level	Conditioning	Parameters
Field	Yes	1) Message ID
		2) Message file
		3) Response indicator (optional)
		4) Message data (optional)

This keyword displays an error message from a message file for a specified field.

PARAMETER DEFINITIONS

Message ID

This parameter is the seven-character identifier of the message to be displayed.

Message file

This parameter is the name of the message file that contains the message ID. You can qualify the file name with the name of the library if you wish.

Response indicator

This optional parameter is used to turn off an indicator (normally the same indicator specified in the conditioning columns) when control is returned to your HLL program.

Message data

This optional parameter is used to pass data from your HLL program to the message identifier. The field name must be defined within the same record format and have a data type of A and a usage of P. The length of the field depends on the message ID requirements.

```
....1....+....2....+....3....+....4....+....5....+....6....+....7....+....8
A                     R FORMAT1
A                       CUSNBR          7S 0B 10 10
A  70                                              ERRMSGID(USR0020 USERMSGF)
A                       CUSNAM         35A  B 10 20
A  71                                              ERRMSGID(USR0021 PRODLIB/USERMSGF +
A                                                  71 &DATA)
A                       DATA           10A  P
```

ERRSFL (Error Subfile)

Level	Conditioning	Parameters
File	No	None

This keyword creates an automatic error-message subfile on the screen to show all error messages generated for the screen. This subfile is not the same as a user-created error-message subfile.

When you use the ERRSFL keyword, all error messages are shown within the subfile and the keyboard is not locked.

```
....1....+....2....+....3....+....4....+....5....+....6....+....7....+....8
A                                                  ERRSFL
A                     R FORMAT1
A                       CUSNBR          7S 0B 10 10
A  70                                              ERRMSG('Invalid customer #')
A                       CUSNAM         35A  B 10 20
A  71                                              ERRMSG('Name cannot be blank' 71)
```

FLDCSRPRG (Field Cursor Progression)

Level	Conditioning	Parameters
Field	No	1) Field name

This keyword specifies the name of the field to which the cursor is to be moved when the user exits a field.

PARAMETER DEFINITION

Field name

This parameter is the name of the field to which the cursor is to be moved. The field must be defined within the same record format.

```
....1....+....2....+....3....+....4....+....5....+....6....+....7....+....8
A                     R FORMAT1
A                       FIELD1         10A  B 10 10FLDCSRPRG(FIELD3)
A                       FIELD2         10A  B 10 20FLDCSRPRG(FIELD1)
A                       FIELD3         10A  B 11 20FLDCSRPRG(FIELD2)
```

FLTFIXDEC (Floating-Point to Fixed-Decimal)

Level	Conditioning	Parameters
Field	No	None

This keyword displays a floating-point number in fixed-decimal notation. The number is displayed in fixed-decimal notation only if the value is small enough; otherwise, it is displayed in standard floating-point form.

```
....1....+....2....+....3....+....4....+....5....+....6....+....7....+....8
A               R FORMAT1
A                 FIELD1        8F 3  10 10FLTFIXDEC
```

FLTPCN (Floating-Point Precision)

Level	Conditioning	Parameters
Field	No	1) Precision

This keyword specifies the precision or size of a floating-point number when the number is displayed.

PARAMETER DEFINITION

Precision
This parameter is a value of *SINGLE or *DOUBLE. *SINGLE floating-point numbers can be up to nine digits long. *DOUBLE floating-point numbers can be up to 17 digits long.

```
....1....+....2....+....3....+....4....+....5....+....6....+....7....+....8
A               R FORMAT1
A                 FIELD1       17F 5  10 10FLTPCN(*DOUBLE)
```

FRCDTA (Force Data)

Level	Conditioning	Parameters
Field	No	1) Precision

This keyword force-sends the record format to the screen when the format is written with no associated read request (i.e., using WRITE instead of EXFMT in RPG). FRCDTA overrides the DFRWRT(*YES) parameter on the CRTDSPF and CHGDSPF commands.

```
....1....+....2....+....3....+....4....+....5....+....6....+....7....+....8
A               R FORMAT1
A                                          FRCDTA
A                 CUSNBR        7S 0  10 10
A                 CUSNAM       35A     10 20
```

GETRETAIN (Get Retain)

Level	Conditioning	Parameters
Record	No	None

This keyword is used in connection with the UNLOCK keyword to prevent input-capable fields on the screen from being cleared.

```
....1....+....2....+....3....+....4....+....5....+....6....+....7....+....8
A          R FORMAT1
A                                             UNLOCK
A                                             GETRETAIN
A            CUSNBR        7S 0B 10 10
A            CUSNAM       35A  B 10 20
```

HELP (Help)

Level	Conditioning	Parameters
File	Yes	1) Response indicator (optional)
Record		2) Text (optional)

This keyword enables the Help key. The Help key acts like a command attention key in that all screen validity checking is bypassed.

If online Help is defined for this display file and the Help key is pressed, online Help is displayed. Otherwise, control is returned to the HLL program.

PARAMETER DEFINITIONS

Response indicator
This optional parameter specifies the indicator number to be turned on when the user presses the Help key. The valid values are 01 to 99.

Text
The text parameter contains up to 50 characters of text to serve as documentation for the keyword. You code the text within apostrophes (').

```
....1....+....2....+....3....+....4....+....5....+....6....+....7....+....8
A                                         HELP(28 'Help requested')
A          R FORMAT1
A            CUSNBR        7S 0  10 10
A            CUSNAM       35A    10 20
```

HLPARA (Help Area)

Level	Conditioning	Parameters
Help	No	There are five parameter settings, depending on the kind of help area being defined.
		Explicit Help Area: 1) Top row 2) Top column 3) Bottom row 4) Bottom column
		Record Format Area: 1) Help qualifier
		No Help Area: 1) Help qualifier
		Field Level Help Area: 1) Help qualifier 2) Field name 3) Choice number (optional)
		Constant Level Help Area: 1) Help qualifier 2) Help identifier

This keyword defines a rectangular box on the screen for which online help is made available. The HLPARA keyword must be specified somewhere within a Help specification. You define a Help specification by placing an H in column 17.

You can specify more than one HLPARA keyword per record format. However, the order in which you specify the help areas is important — you should specify them from smallest area to largest area.

HLPARA also lets you use conditioning names (see the DSPSIZ keyword) when multiple screen sizes are available so you can define different help areas based on the screen size being used.

Five types of help areas can be defined:

- an explicit rectangular box defined by the programmer

- the entire area covered by the record format

- the area associated with a specific field/choice

- the area associated with some constant data on the screen

- a help area not associated with an area on the screen

The parameter settings depend on the type of area you're defining.

Parameter Definitions: Explicit Help Area

Top row
This parameter is the row number of the upper left corner of the help area being defined.

Top column
This parameter is the column number of the upper left corner of the help area being defined.

Bottom row
This parameter is the row number of the lower right corner of the help area being defined.

Bottom column
This parameter is the column number of the lower right corner of the help area being defined.

Parameter Definition: Record Format Help Area

Help qualifier
This parameter is a value of *RCD, indicating that the help area is defined by the first line in the record format to the last line in the record format.

Parameter Definition: No Help Area

Help qualifier
This parameter is a value of *NONE, indicating that online help is not associated with any area on the screen. Users see online help only if they roll to that help information.

Parameter Definitions: Field Level Help Area

Help qualifier
This parameter is a value of *FLD, indicating that the online help is associated with a specific field.

Field name
This parameter is the name of the field for which online help is available. The field name must exist within the record format.

Choice number
This optional parameter lets you specify the particular choice number that has online help when the field is a single- or multiple-choice field.

PARAMETER DEFINITIONS: CONSTANT LEVEL HELP AREA

Help qualifier

This parameter is a value of *CNST, indicating that the online help is associated with some constant in the record format.

Help identifier

This parameter is a number associated with some constant in the record format. The number is defined by the HLPID keyword.

```
....1....+....2....+....3....+....4....+....5....+....6....+....7....+....8
A                                           HELP
A            R FORMAT1
A            H                              HLPARA(*CNST 1)
A                                           HLPRCD(HELPFMT1)
A            H                              HLPARA(*FLD EMPNAM)
A                                           HLPRCD(HELPFMT2)
A            H                              HLPARA(*FLD MRTSTS 2)
A                                           HLPRCD(HELPFMT3)
A            H                              HLPARA(*RCD)
A                                           HLPRCD(HELPFMT4)
A            H                              HLPARA(1 1 24 80)
A                                           HLPRCD(HELPFMT5)
A            H                              HLPARA(*NONE)
A                                           HLDRCD(HELPFMT6)
A                                        9 10'Employee #'  HLPID(1)
A              EMP#        9S 0  10 10
A              EMPNAM      35A    10 20
A              MRTSTS      1A  B 15 35SNGCHCFLD
A                                           CHOICE(1 'Single')
A                                           CHOICE(2 'Married')
```

HLPBDY (Help Boundary)

Level	Conditioning	Parameters
Help	No	None

HLPBDY lets you control what online help is available at any given time by setting boundaries for displaying online help. All help areas defined up to and including the one containing the HLPBDY keyword are available to the user.

```
....1....+....2....+....3....+....4....+....5....+....6....+....7....+....8
A                                           HELP
A            R FORMAT1
A            H                              HLPARA(*CNST 1)
A                                           HLPRCD(HELPFMT1)
A                                           HLPBDY
A            H                              HLPARA(*FLD EMPNAM)
A                                           HLPRCD(HELPFMT2)
A                                           HLPBDY
A            H                              HLPARA(*FLD MRTSTS 2)
A                                           HLPRCD(HELPFMT3)
A                                           HLPBDY
A            H                              HLPARA(*RCD)
A                                           HLPRCD(HELPFMT4)
A            H                              HLPARA(1 1 24 80)
```

```
....1....+....2....+....3....+....4....+....5....+....6....+....7....+....8
A                                             HLPRCD(HELPFMT5)
A          H                                  HLPARA(*NONE)
A                                             HLDRCD(HELPFMT6)
A                                       9 10'Employee #'  HLPID(1)
A          EMP#           9S 0  10 10
A          EMPNAM        35A    10 20
A          MRTSTS         1A  B 15 35SNGCHCFLD
A                                             CHOICE(1 'Single')
A                                             CHOICE(2 'Married')
```

HLPCLR (Help Clear)

Level	Conditioning	Parameters
Record	Yes	None

This keyword clears all currently active help areas on the screen, making the only active help areas those defined in the record format.

```
....1....+....2....+....3....+....4....+....5....+....6....+....7....+....8
A                                             HELP
A          R FORMAT1
A   40                                        HLPCLR
A          H                                  HLPARA(*RCD)
A                                             HLPRCD(HELPFMT4)
A          H                                  HLPARA(1 1 24 80)
A                                             HLPRCD(HELPFMT5)
A          CUSNBR         7S 0  10 10
A          CUSNAM        35A    10 20
```

HLPCMDKEY (Help Command Key)

Level	Conditioning	Parameters
Record	No	None

This keyword returns control to your HLL program when the user presses a command attention (CAnn) or command function (CFnn) key defined on a record format being used as online help.

```
....1....+....2....+....3....+....4....+....5....+....6....+....7....+....8
A                                             HELP
A          R FORMAT1
A          H                                  HLPARA(1 1 24 80)
A                                             HLPRCD(HELPFMT5)
A          CUSNBR         7S 0  10 10
A          CUSNAM        35A    10 20
A          R HELPFMT5                          HLPCMDKEY
A                                             CA03(03 'Exit')
A                                       23  2'F3=Return Application'
```

HLPDOC (Help Document)

Level	Conditioning	Parameters
File Help	Yes	1) Label name
		2) Document name
		3) Folder name

This keyword specifies the OfficeVision/400 document to be used as online help. When you specify this keyword at the file level, it acts as the default online help for the display file when no other help is defined for a specific area on the screen.

PARAMETER DEFINITIONS

Label name
This parameter is the name of a help label defined in the OV/400 document. The online help is positioned to this point in the document.

Document name
This parameter is the name of the OV/400 document to use as online help.

Folder name
This parameter is the name of the folder that contains the OV/400 document.

```
....1....+....2....+....3....+....4....+....5....+....6....+....7....+....8
A                                       HELP
A          R FORMAT1
A          H                            HLPARA(1 1 24 80)
A                                       HLPDOC(BEGIN OVERVIEW.HLP HELP.FLR)
A            CUSNBR        7S 0   10 10
A            CUSNAM        35A     10 20
```

HLPEXCLD (Help Exclude)

Level	Conditioning	Parameters
Help	Yes	None

This keyword indicates that the online help being defined is not to be used as extended help. The help is available only when the user specifically requests help for the defined help area. This keyword is used in connection with UIM help panels only (see the HLPPNLGRP keyword).

```
....1....+....2....+....3....+....4....+....5....+....6....+....7....+....8
A                                       HELP
A          R FORMAT1
A          H                            HLPARA(1 1 24 80)
A                                       HLPPNLGRP(NAME1 GROUP1)
A                                       HLPEXCLD
A            CUSNBR        7S 0   10 10
A            CUSNAM        35A     10 20
```

HLPFULL (Help Full)

Level	Conditioning	Parameters
File	No	None

This keyword indicates that all UIM help panels are to be displayed using the full screen instead of windows.

```
....1....+....2....+....3....+....4....+....5....+....6....+....7....+....8
A                                               HELP
A                                               HLPFULL
A          R FORMAT1
A          H                                    HLPARA(1 1 24 80)
A                                               HLPPNLGRP(NAME1 GROUP1)
A            CUSNBR          7S 0  10 10
A            CUSNAM         35A     10 20
```

HLPID (Help Identifier)

Level	Conditioning	Parameters
Field	No	1) Help identifier

This keyword assigns a help identifier (number) with some specific constant text in a record format, letting you specify online help for text displayed on the screen.

```
....1....+....2....+....3....+....4....+....5....+....6....+....7....+....8
A                                               HELP
A          R FORMAT1
A          H                                    HLPARA(*CNST 1)
A                                               HLPRCD(HELPFMT5)
A                              9 10'Customer #'
A                                               HLPID(1)
A            CUSNBR          7S 0  10 10
A            CUSNAM         35A     10 20
```

HLPPNLGRP (Help Panel Group)

Level	Conditioning	Parameters
File Help	Yes	1) Module name
		2) Panel group

This keyword specifies the UIM help panel to be used as online help. When you specify this keyword at the file level, it acts as the default online help for the display file when no Help is defined for a specific area on the screen.

When you use HLPPNLGRP in a display file, the display file cannot contain either the HLPRCD or the HLPDOC keyword.

PARAMETER DEFINITIONS

Module name

This parameter is the name of the panel-group help module to be displayed as online help.

Panel group

This parameter is the name of the UIM panel group that contains the help module name.

```
....1....+....2....+....3....+....4....+....5....+....6....+....7....+....8
A                                           HELP
A            R FORMAT1
A            H                              HLPARA(1 1 24 80)
A                                           HLPPNLGRP(NAME1 GROUP1)
A              CUSNBR       7S 0   10 10
A              CUSNAM       35A    10 20
```

HLPRCD (Help Record)

Level	Conditioning	Parameters
File Help	Yes	1) Format name
		2) File name (optional)

This keyword specifies the name of a record format in some file that will be used as online help. When you specify this keyword at the file level, it acts as the default online help for the display file when no help is defined for a specific area on the screen.

PARAMETER DEFINITIONS

Format name

This parameter is the name of the record format to be used as online help.

File name

This optional parameter specifies the name of the file that contains the record format. The default is to use the same display file. You can optionally specify the name of the library in which the file is located.

```
....1....+....2....+....3....+....4....+....5....+....6....+....7....+....8
A                                           HELP
A            R FORMAT1
A            H                              HLPARA(5 5 10 10)
A                                           HLPRCD(HELPFMT1)
A            H                              HLPARA(1 1 24 80)
A                                           HLPRCD(HELPFMT9 HELPFILE)
A              CUSNBR       7S 0   10 10
A              CUSNAM       35A    10 20
```

HLPRTN (Help Return)

Level	Conditioning	Parameters
File	Yes	1) Response indicator
Record		2) Text

When online help is available, this keyword returns control to your HLL program when the help key is pressed. The HLPRTN keyword overrides the HLPRCD, HLPDOC, and HLPPNLGRP keywords.

PARAMETER DEFINITIONS

Response indicator
This optional parameter specifies the indicator to be turned on when the user presses the help key. The valid values are 01 to 99.

Text
The text parameter contains up to 50 characters of text to serve as documentation for the keyword. You code the text within apostrophes (').

```
....1....+....2....+....3....+....4....+....5....+....6....+....7....+....8
A                                        HELP
A           R FORMAT1
A    40
A           H                            HLPRTN
A                                        HLPARA(5 5 10 10)
A                                        HLPRCD(HELPFMT1)
A                CUSNBR        7S 0   10 10
A                CUSNAM        35A    10 20
```

HLPSCHIDX (Help Search Index)

Level	Conditioning	Parameters
File	No	1) Search index

This keyword enables the use of the index search function (F11) when online help is displayed. You use this keyword in connection with UIM help panels only.

HLPSCHIDX cannot be used with the HLPSHELF keyword; they are mutually exclusive.

PARAMETER DEFINITION

Search index
This parameter is the name of the search index object to be used for the F11 function. You can optionally specify the name of the library in which the search index is located.

```
....1....+....2....+....3....+....4....+....5....+....6....+....7....+....8
A                                          HELP
A                                          HLPSCHIDX(INDEX1)
A          R FORMAT1
A          H                               HLPARA(5 5 10 10)
A                                          HLPPNLGRP(NAME1 GROUP1)
A            CUSNBR       7S 0  10 10
A            CUSNAM      35A    10 20
```

HLPSEQ (Help Sequence)

Level	Conditioning	Parameters
Record	No	1) Group name
		2) Sequence number

You use this keyword in connection with record-format help to link multiple record formats with a single help area so you are not limited to a single screen of help text when you use record-format help.

PARAMETER DEFINITIONS

Group name
This parameter is a name from 1 to 10 characters long used to identify a unique help group.

Sequence number
This parameter is a number from 0 to 99 that orders the record formats in the help group and determines the order in which they are presented to the user.

```
....1....+....2....+....3....+....4....+....5....+....6....+....7....+....8
A                                          HELP
A          R FORMAT1
A          H                               HLPARA(5 5 10 10)
A                                          HLPRCD(HELPFMT1)
A            CUSNBR       7S 0  10 10
A            CUSNAM      35A    10 20
A          R HELPFMT1                       HLPSEQ(HGROUP1 0)
A                                     1 2'Help format #1'
A          R HELPFMT2                       HLPSEQ(HGROUP1 1)
```

HLPSHELF (Help Bookshelf)

Level	Conditioning	Parameters
File	No	1) Bookshelf

This keyword enables the use of the Infoseeker function (F11) when online help is displayed. You use this keyword in connection with UIM help panels only. The HLPSCHIDX keyword cannot be used with HLPSHELF.

PARAMETER DEFINITION

Bookshelf

This parameter is the name of the bookshelf object in the user's bookpath to be used for the Infoseeker function. You can specify a value of *LIST to display the list of bookshelves in the user's bookpath.

```
....1....+....2....+....3....+....4....+....5....+....6....+....7....+....8
A                                         HELP
A                                         HLPSHELF(BOOK1)
A          R FORMAT1
A          H                              HLPARA(5 5 10 10)
A                                         HLPPNLGRP(NAME1 GROUP1)
A            CUSNBR      7S 0  10 10
A            CUSNAM     35A    10 20
```

HLPTITLE (Help Title)

Level	Conditioning	Parameters
File	Yes	1) Text
Record		

This keyword specifies the default title of a UIM help panel that is displayed in full-screen mode.

PARAMETER DEFINITION

Text

This parameter is a text string of up to 55 characters embedded within apostrophes (').

```
....1....+....2....+....3....+....4....+....5....+....6....+....7....+....8
A                                         HELP
A                                         HLPTITLE('Help Panel #1')
A          R FORMAT1
A          H                              HLPARA(5 5 10 10)
A                                         HLPPNLGRP(NAME1 GROUP1)
A            CUSNBR      7S 0  10 10
A            CUSNAM     35A    10 20
```

HOME (Home)

Level	Conditioning	Parameters
File	Yes	1) Response indicator (optional)
Record		2) Text (optional)

This keyword causes the Home key to return control to the HLL program. The Home key acts like a command attention key by causing all screen validity checking to be bypassed. Control is returned only when the cursor is at the "home" position on the screen.

PARAMETER DEFINITIONS

Response indicator
This optional parameter specifies the indicator to be turned on when the user presses the Home key. The valid values are from 01 to 99.

Text
The text parameter contains up to 50 characters of text to serve as documentation for the keyword. You code the text within apostrophes (').

```
....1....+....2....+....3....+....4....+....5....+....6....+....7....+....8
A           R FORMAT1
A    40                              HOME(27 'Home key pressed')
A              CUSNBR         7S 0  10 10
A              CUSNAM        35A     10 20
```

HTML (Hypertext Markup Language)

Level	Conditioning	Parameters
Field	Yes	1) Markup text

This keyword sends embedded Hypertext Markup Language tags to the 5250 data stream. When the data is sent to an AS/400 5250 Workstation Gateway device, the appropriate attributes are displayed.

PARAMETER DEFINITION

Markup text
This parameter contains the HTML value to be processed. This parameter either can be a hard-coded value or can be defined by a program-to-system field.

```
....1....+....2....+....3....+....4....+....5....+....6....+....7....+....8
A           R FORMAT1
A                              7 20HTML('<TITLE>')
```

INDARA (Indicator Area)

Level	Conditioning	Parameters
File	No	None

This keyword sets up a separate 99-byte indicator buffer. All indicators used by a record format are placed into this buffer instead of being sent with the record format. INDARA is mainly used by Cobol programs.

```
....1....+....2....+....3....+....4....+....5....+....6....+....7....+....8
A                                                   INDARA
A              R FORMAT1
A     01           CUSNBR        7S 0   10 10
A                  CUSNAM        35A    10 20
```

INDTXT (Indicator Text)

Level	Conditioning	Parameters
File	No	1) Indicator
Record		2) Indicator text

This keyword documents how an indicator is used; it serves no purpose other than documentation.

PARAMETER DEFINITIONS

Indicator
This parameter is a number from 01 to 99.

Indicator text
This parameter is a description of up to 50 characters enclosed by apostrophes (').

```
....1....+....2....+....3....+....4....+....5....+....6....+....7....+....8
A              R FORMAT1
A                                       INDTXT(40 'Display customer #')
A     40           CUSNBR        7S 0   10 10
A                  CUSNAM        35A    10 20
```

INVITE (Invite)

Level	Conditioning	Parameters
File	Yes	None
Record		

This keyword causes a device to be invited for a later read. You normally use the INVITE keyword in connection with multiple-device programs, time-out processing programs, or with the FRCDTA keyword.

```
....1....+....2....+....3....+....4....+....5....+....6....+....7....+....8
A              R FORMAT1
A                                       FRCDTA
A                                       INVITE
A                  CUSNBR        7S 0B 10 10
A                  CUSNAM        35A  B 10 20
```

INZINP (Initialize Input)

Parameter	Conditioning	Parameters
Record	Yes	None

You use this keyword in connection with the PUTOVR and ERASEINP(*ALL) keywords to initialize input fields without necessarily sending the data to the screen.

```
....1....+....2....+....3....+....4....+....5....+....6....+....7....+....8
A             R FORMAT1
A                                              PUTOVR
A    40                                        ERASEINP(*ALL)
A    40                                        INZINP
A               CUSNBR          7S 0B 10 10
A                                              OVRDTA
A               CUSNAM         35A  B 10 20
```

INZRCD (Initialize Record)

Level	Conditioning	Parameters
Record	No	None

This keyword sends the record format to the screen when your HLL program performs a read-only (no output) operation against the record format and that record format is not already on the screen. All fields contain blanks and zeros.

```
....1....+....2....+....3....+....4....+....5....+....6....+....7....+....8
A             R FORMAT1
A                                        INZRCD
A               CUSNBR          7S 0B 10 10
A               CUSNAM         35A  B 10 20
```

KEEP (Keep)

Level	Conditioning	Parameters
Record	No	None

This keyword prevents the current record format, when displayed, from being cleared from the screen when the display file is closed.

```
....1....+....2....+....3....+....4....+....5....+....6....+....7....+....8
A             R FORMAT1
A                                        KEEP
A               CUSNBR          7S 0  10 10
A               CUSNAM         35A     10 20
```

LOCK (Lock)

Level	Conditioning	Parameters
Record	Yes	None

This keyword locks the keyboard after an output operation to the screen. Normally, the keyboard is unlocked when an output operation is performed.

```
....1....+....2....+....3....+....4....+....5....+....6....+....7....+....8
A          R FORMAT1
A                                              LOCK
A                                          5  1'Work is being done.....please wait'
```

LOGINP (Log Input)

Level	Conditioning	Parameters
Record	No	None

This keyword writes the input buffer contents for the record format to the job log every time your HLL program receives data from the screen.

```
....1....+....2....+....3....+....4....+....5....+....6....+....7....+....8
A          R FORMAT1
A                                                  LOGINP
A            CUSNBR        7S 0B 10 10
A            CUSNAM       35A  B 10 20
```

LOGOUT (Log Output)

Level	Conditioning	Parameters
Record	Yes	None

This keyword writes the contents of the output buffer for the record format to the job log every time the HLL program outputs data to the screen.

```
....1....+....2....+....3....+....4....+....5....+....6....+....7....+....8
A          R FORMAT1
A                                                  LOGOUT
A            CUSNBR        7S 0B 10 10
A            CUSNAM       35A  B 10 20
```

LOWER (Lower)

Level	Conditioning	Parameters
Field	No	None

This keyword is the same as the CHECK(LC) keyword. The LOWER keyword lets users enter lowercase characters into an input-capable character field. CHECK(LC) is the preferred choice.

```
....1....+....2....+....3....+....4....+....5....+....6....+....7....+....8
A          R FORMAT1
A            CUSNBR        7S 0B 10 10
A            CUSNAM       35A  B 10 20LOWER
```

MAPVAL (Map Values)

Level	Conditioning	Parameter
Field	No	1) Program value 1
		2) System value 1... Up to 100 combinations

This keyword explicitly changes the value of a field on input and output operations and is valid only on date (L), time (T), and timestamp (Z) fields.

PARAMETER DEFINITIONS

Program value
This parameter can be either an explicit value or a special value of *BLANK or *CUR. *BLANK indicates that the program value contains a blank. *CUR specifies that the date, time, or timestamp is the current field data.

System value
This parameter can be either an explicit value or a special value of *BLANK or *CUR. *BLANK indicates that the program value contains a blank. *CUR specifies that the date, time, or timestamp is the current field data.

```
....1....+....2....+....3....+....4....+....5....+....6....+....7....+....8
A              R FORMAT1
A                FIELD1        L     10 10DATFMT(*YMD)
A                                       MAPVAL(('40/01/01' *BLANK))h
```

MDTOFF (Modified Data Tag Off)

Level	Conditioning	Parameters
Record	Yes	1) Input choice (optional)

You use this keyword in connection with the OVERLAY keyword to turn off the modified data tag for input-capable fields. This keyword affects those input fields already on the screen when the record format is written; it does not affect the fields in the record format.

PARAMETER DEFINITION

Input choice
This optional parameter indicates which input fields are to have their modified data tags turned off. The valid values are *UNPR and *ALL. *UNPR, the default, affects only unprotected input-capable fields. *ALL affects every input-capable field on the screen.

```
....1....+....2....+....3....+....4....+....5....+....6....+....7....+....8
A          R FORMAT1
A                                                      OVERLAY
A                                                      MDTOFF(*ALL)
A            CUSNBR         7S 0B 10 10
A            CUSNAM        35A  B 10 20
```

MLTCHCFLD (Multiple Choice Field)

Level	Conditioning	Parameters
Field	No	1) Restrict cursor (optional)
		2) Selection indicator (optional)
		3) Column row (optional)
		4) Gutter (optional)

This keyword defines a field as a multiple-choice field.

PARAMETER DEFINITIONS

Restrict cursor

This optional parameter indicates whether to allow the user to move the cursor outside of the field-defined choice area. The values are *RSTCSR and *NORSTCSR. *RSTCSR prevents the user from moving the cursor outside of the choice area. *NORSTCSR lets the user move the cursor and is the default.

Selection indicator

This optional parameter indicates whether the selection indicators (i.e., check boxes) should be displayed. The valid values are *SLTIND and *NOSLTIND. *SLTIND is the default and shows the selection indicators. *NOSLTIND does not show the selection indicators.

Column row

This optional parameter defines how the choices are displayed (in multiple columns or multiple rows. The format of this parameter is either (*NUMCOL number) or (*NUMROW number). For each definition, you enter the number of columns or rows to be used.

Displaying the choices in multiple columns causes the choices to appear in left-to-right, top-to-bottom order:

```
choice1   choice2   choice3
choice4   choice5   choice6
```

Displaying the choices in multiple rows causes them to appear from top to bottom, then left to right, in multiple columns:

```
choice1   choice3   choice5
choice2   choice4   choice6
```

Gutter

If you specify *NUMCOL or *NUMROW, you can also specify this optional parameter. The gutter parameter defines the number of spaces to be used between each choice. The format of this parameter is (*GUTTER number). The number entered must be at least two. The default gutter space is three.

```
....1....+....2....+....3....+....4....+....5....+....6....+....7....+....8
A              R FORMAT1
A                FIELD1        2Y 0B  1  2MLTCHCFLD(*RSTCSR *NOSLTIND +
A                                          (*NUMCOL 3) (*GUTTER 5))
A                                        CHOICE(1 'Update')
A                                        CHOICE(2 'Add')
A                                        CHOICE(3 'Delete')
A                                        CHCCTL(1 &CHC1)
A                                        CHCCTL(2 &CHC2)
A                                        CHCCTL(3 &CHC3)
A                FIELD2        2Y 0B 10  2MLTCHCFLD
A                                        CHOICE(1 'Choice #1')
A                                        CHOICE(2 'Choice #2')
A                                        CHCCTL(1 &CHC4)
A                                        CHCCTL(2 &CHC5)
A                CHC1          1Y 0H
A                CHC2          1Y 0H
A                CHC3          1Y 0H
A                CHC4          1Y 0H
A                CHC5          1Y 0H
```

MNUBAR (Menu Bar)

Level	Conditioning	Parameters
Record	No	1) Line separator (optional)

This keyword defines a record format as a menu bar.

PARAMETER DEFINITION

Line separator

This optional parameter indicates whether a separator line should be placed on the screen. The valid values are *SEPARATOR (the default) and *NOSEPARATOR.

```
....1....+....2....+....3....+....4....+....5....+....6....+....7....+....8
A              R FORMAT1                    MNUBAR(*NOSEPARATOR)
A                MENU1         2Y 0  1  2
A                                           MNUBARCHC(1 INQFMT 'Inquiry')
A                                           MNUBARCHC(2 MNTFMT 'Maintenance')
```

MNUBARCHC (Menu Bar Choice)

Level	Conditioning	Parameters
Field	Yes	1) Choice number
		2) Record format
		3) Choice text
		4) Return field (optional)

This keyword defines the choices available for a menu bar. The field for which you code MNUBARCHC must be defined with a data type of Y, be two digits long with zero decimal positions, and be placed at row one column two.

PARAMETER DEFINITIONS

Choice number

This parameter is a number from 01 to 99. Each choice must have a unique number assigned.

Record format

This parameter is the name of a pull-down record format within the same display file.

Choice text

This parameter is the text to be shown for the menu bar choice. You can either hard-code this parameter in the DDS or use a variable field. If you use a variable field, you must define that field in the same record format and it must have a data type of A and a usage of P.

You can also specify a mnemonic for the menu bar choice in the text. You do this by placing a > character before the character that will act as the mnemonic. The designated character appears on the screen underlined.

Return field

This optional parameter specifies that control is to be returned to the HLL program when the user selects this choice. The value of the option is placed into the field when control is returned to the program. This field must be defined within the same record format, have a data type of Y, be 2 digits long with 0 decimals, and have a usage of H.

```
....1....+....2....+....3....+....4....+....5....+....6....+....7....+....8
A          R FORMAT1                    MNUBAR
A            MENU1         2Y 0B  1  2
A                                       MNUBARCHC(1 INQFMT '>Inquiry')
A                                       MNUBARCHC(2 MNTFMT '>Maintenance')
A                                       MNUBARCHC(3 OPTFMT &OPTION)
A                                       MNUBARCHC(4 HLPFMT '>Help' &RTNCHC)
A            OPTION       15A  P
A            RTNCHC        2Y 0H
```

MNUBARDSP (Menu Bar Display)

Level	Conditioning	Parameters
Record	Yes	NOTE: The parameters for this keyword can be defined two ways.
		Referenced Menu Bar:
		1) Menu bar format
		2) Choice field
		3) Pull-down value (optional)
		Within Menu Bar:
		1) Pull-down value (optional)

This keyword controls when a menu bar is displayed. You can specify this keyword in two ways.

One option is to specify this keyword in the same record format as the MNUBAR keyword.

Alternatively, you can put the keyword in a format that references a menu bar. When the record format is displayed with the MNUBARDSP keyword active, the reference menu bar is displayed.

PARAMETER DEFINITIONS: REFERENCED MENU BAR

Menu bar format
This parameter is the name of the menu-bar record format to be displayed.

Choice field
This parameter is a field that contains the number of the menu-bar choice the user has made. The field must be defined within the same record format, have a data type of Y, be two digits long with zero decimal positions, and have a usage of H.

Pull-down value
This optional parameter specifies a field name that contains the choice the user selected from the specific pull-down menu.

When the value returned is 0, the user made no selection. When the value returned is -1, the user did something other than make a single choice; you must read the pull-down-record format to find out what choices the user made.

The field must be defined within the same record format, have a data type of S, be two digits long with zero decimal positions, and have a usage of H.

PARAMETER DEFINITION: WITHIN MENU BAR

Pull-down value

This optional parameter specifies a field name that contains the choice the user selected from the pull-down menu defined with the menu bar.

When a value of 0 is returned, the user made no selection. When the value returned is -1, the user did something other than make a single choice; you must read the pull-down record format to determine what choices the user made.

The field must be defined within the same record format, have a data type of S, be two digits long with zero decimal positions, and have a usage of H.

```
....1....+....2....+....3....+....4....+....5....+....6....+....7....+....8
A          R FORMAT1
A   40                                   MNUBARDSP(MENUFMT &MNUCHC &PULOPT)
A            MNUCHC        2Y ØH
A            PULOPT        2S ØH
A          R MENUFMT
A                                        MNUBAR
A            MENU1         2Y ØB   1  2
A                                        MNUBARCHC(1 INQFMT '>Inquiry')
A                                        MNUBARCHC(2 MNTFMT '>Maintenance')
A          R FORMAT1
A                                        MNUBAR
A                                        MNUBARDSP
A            MENU1         2Y ØB   1  2
A                                        MNUBARCHC(1 INQFMT '>Inquiry')
A                                        MNUBARCHC(2 MNTFMT '>Maintenance')
```

MNUBARSEP (Menu Bar Separator)

Level	Conditioning	Parameters
Field	Yes	1) Color (optional)
		2) Display attribute (optional)
		3) Character (optional)
		NOTE: You must specify at least one of these parameters.

This keyword defines how the menu-bar separator line is to appear on the screen.

PARAMETER DEFINITIONS

Color

This parameter specifies the color to be used for the separator line. The Color parameter has two elements: *COLOR and one of the following color identifiers:

- (*COLOR GRN)   Green
- (*COLOR RED)   Red
- (*COLOR BLU)   Blue

- (*COLOR WHT)   White
- (*COLOR TRQ)   Turquoise
- (*COLOR YLW)   Yellow
- (*COLOR PNK)   Pink

The default color is blue.

Display attribute
This parameter specifies which display attribute is to be used for the separator line. This parameter has two elements: *DSPATR and one of the following display attributes:

- (*DSPATR BL)   Blink
- (*DSPATR CS)   Column Separator
- (*DSPATR HI)   High Intensity
- (*DSPATR ND)   Non-Display
- (*DSPATR RI)   Reverse Image
- (*DSPATR UL)   Underline

You can specify more than one display attribute after the *DSPATR code; for example, (*DSPATR HI RI). The default display attribute is normal video.

Character
This parameter defines the character to be used to make up the separator line. The Character parameter has two elements: *CHAR and a single character specified within apostrophes (e.g., (*CHAR '-')). The default value is a dash (-).

```
....1....+....2....+....3....+....4....+....5....+....6....+....7....+....8
A          R FORMAT1
A                                    MNUBAR
A            MENU1        2Y 0B  1  2
A                                    MNUBARSEP((*COLOR RED)   +
A                                    (*DSPATR HI) (*CHAR '='))
A                                    MNUBARCHC(1 INQFMT '>Inquiry')
A                                    MNUBARCHC(2 MNTFMT '>Maintenance')
```

MNUBARSW (Menu Bar Switch Key)

Level	Conditioning	Parameters
File	Yes	1) Command key (optional)
Record		

This keyword specifies a command attention key the user can press to switch between a menu bar and an application screen. The MNUBARSW keyword is used in connection with referenced menu bar displays (see the MNUBARDSP keyword).

PARAMETER DEFINITION

Command key

This optional parameter specifies the command attention key used for the switch function. The valid values are CA01 to CA24. The default is CA10.

```
....1....+....2....+....3....+....4....+....5....+....6....+....7....+....8
A                                    MNUBARSW(CA07)
A         R FORMAT1
A   40                               MNUBARDSP(MENUFMT &MNUCHC &PULOPT)
A           MNUCHC       2Y 0H
A           PULOPT       2S 0H
A         R MENUFMT
A                                    MNUBAR
A           MENU1        2Y 0B  1  2
A                                    MNUBARCHC(1 INQFMT '>Inquiry')
A                                    MNUBARCHC(2 MNTFMT '>Maintenance')
```

MNUCNL (Menu Cancel)

Level	Conditioning	Parameters
File	Yes	1) Command key (optional)
Record		2) Response indicator (optional)

This keyword specifies a command key the user can press to cancel a pull-down menu, return to an application screen, or return control to the HLL program. The action that takes place when the key is pressed depends on where the cursor is positioned and which options are active.

PARAMETER DEFINITIONS

Command key

This optional parameter specifies the command key to be used for the cancel function. The valid values are CA01 to CA24. The default is CA12.

Response indicator

This optional parameter is allowed when you specify the command key parameter. The response indicator is a number from 01 to 99 that corresponds to the indicator to be turned on when control is returned to the HLL program.

```
....1....+....2....+....3....+....4....+....5....+....6....+....7....+....8
A                                    MNUCNL(CA15)
A         R FORMAT1
A   40                               MNUBARDSP(MENUFMT &MNUCHC &PULOPT)
A           MNUCHC       2Y 0H
A           PULOPT       2S 0H
A         R MENUFMT
A                                    MNUBAR
A           MENU1        2Y 0B  1  2
A                                    MNUBARCHC(1 INQFMT '>Inquiry')
A                                    MNUBARCHC(2 MNTFMT '>Maintenance')
```

MOUBTN (Mouse Button)

Level	Conditioning	Parameters
File	Yes	1) Event
Record		2) Trailing event (optional)
		3) Command key
		4) Queue

This keyword associates a command key or event with the use of a pointer device such as a mouse.

PARAMETER DEFINITIONS

Event

This parameter is a value that indicates which mouse event is being defined. The valid values for this parameter and their meanings are shown in the table that follows.

Code	Meaning
*ULP	Unshifted left button pressed
*ULR	Unshifted left button released
*ULD	Unshifted left button double click
*UMP	Unshifted middle button pressed
*UMR	Unshifted middle button released
*UMD	Unshifted middle button double click
*URP	Unshifted right button pressed
*URR	Unshifted right button released
*URD	Unshifted right button double click
*SLP	Shifted left button pressed
*SLR	Shifted left button released
*SLD	Shifted left button double click
*SMP	Shifted middle button pressed
*SMR	Shifted middle button released
*SMD	Shifted middle button double click
*SRP	Shifted right button pressed
*SRR	Shifted right button released
*SRD	Shifted right button double click

Trailing event

This optional parameter associates a command key with two mouse events. The valid values are the same as for the event parameter.

Command key

This parameter is the command key or event to be invoked when the user selects the defined mouse event. The valid values and their meanings are listed below.

Code	Meaning
CA01-CA24	Command attention keys 1-24
CF01-CF24	Command function keys 1-24
E00-E15	Event ID (similar to CAnn keys)
ENTER	Enter key
HELP	Help key
HOME	Home key
PRINT	Print key
CLEAR	Clear key
ROLLUP	Roll-up request
ROLLDOWN	Roll-down request

Queue

This optional parameter indicates whether the workstation controller should queue a single event if it is received while the keyboard is locked. The valid values are *QUEUE and *NOQUEUE. The default is *NOQUEUE.

```
....1....+....2....+....3....+....4....+....5....+....6....+....7....+....8
A           R FORMAT1
A     40                                      MOUBTN(*ULD CA05 *QUEUE)
A     41                                      MOUBTN(*SLP *SLR CF04)
A           CUSNBR        7S 0B 10 10
A           CUSNAM       35A  B 10 20
```

MSGALARM (Message Alarm)

Level	Conditioning	Parameters
File	Yes	None
Record		

This keyword sounds an audible alarm at the workstation when an active error message is generated. The active error message can be caused by the ERRMSG, ERRMSGID, SFLMSG, or SFLMSGID keyword or by any validity-checking keyword.

```
....1....+....2....+....3....+....4....+....5....+....6....+....7....+....8
A           R FORMAT1
A     40                                      MSGALARM
A           CUSNBR        7S 0B 10 10
A     70                                      ERRMSG('Invalid Customer #' 70)
A           CUSNAM       35A  B 10 20
```

MSGCON (Message Constant)

Level	Conditioning	Parameters
Field	No	1) Length
		2) Message ID
		3) Message file

This keyword displays text that has been stored in a message file. The message text is linked with the display file at compile time.

PARAMETER DEFINITIONS

Length
This parameter specifies the number of characters to be displayed.

Message ID
This parameter is the seven-character identifier of the message ID that contains the text.

Message file
This parameter is the name of the message file that contains the message ID. You can qualify the file name with the name of the library if you wish.

```
....1....+....2....+....3....+....4....+....5....+....6....+....7....+....8
A          R FORMAT1
A                           10 10MSGCON(10 USR0001 USERMSGF)
```

MSGID (Message Identifier)

Level	Conditioning	Parameters
Field	Yes	1) Message ID
		2) Message file

This keyword displays text that has been stored in a message file. The HLL program links the message text with the display file at runtime.

You code this keyword on a named field. The length of the field determines the amount of text to be displayed.

PARAMETER DEFINITIONS

Message ID
This parameter is the seven-character ID of the message that contains the text. You can define the message ID either explicitly in the DDS or by means of a variable field. When you use a variable field, you can either code a seven-character variable field or use a hard-coded three-character prefix with a four-character variable. The field name must be defined within the same record

format, have a data type of A, be seven or four characters long, and have a usage of H, P, B, or O.

You can specify the special value of *NONE in place of a message ID to indicate that no message text is to be displayed. If you use *NONE, do not specify a message file.

Message file

This parameter is the name of the message file that contains the message ID. You can qualify the file name with the name of the library if you wish. You can also use a variable field to specify the name of the file or library. This field name must be defined within the same record format, have a data type of A, be 10 characters long, and have a usage of H, P, B, or O.

```
....1....+....2....+....3....+....4....+....5....+....6....+....7....+....8
A          R FORMAT1
A            FIELD1        10A     1 10MSGID(USR0005 USERMSGF)
A            FIELD2        15A     2 10MSGID(USR0006 PRODLIB/USERMSGF)
A            FIELD3        12A     3 10MSGID(USR &MSG# USERMSGF)
A            FIELD4         8A     4 10MSGID(&MSGID &MSGF)
A            FIELD5        22A     5 10MSGID(&MSGID &LIB/&MSGF)
A            MSG#           4A  H
A            MSGID          7A  H
A            MSGF          10A  H
A            LIB           10A  H
```

MSGLOC (Message Location)

Level	Conditioning	Parameters
File	No	1) Line number

This keyword specifies the number of the line on which error messages are to appear.

PARAMETER DEFINITION

Line number

This parameter is a number from 01 to 28. The number entered must be valid for the screen sizes the display file uses.

```
....1....+....2....+....3....+....4....+....5....+....6....+....7....+....8
A                                        MSGLOC(23)
A          R FORMAT1
```

NOCCSID (No Coded Character Set Identifier)

Level	Conditioning	Parameters
File	No	None

This keyword specifies that CCSID conversion is not to take place for the field.

```
....1....+....2....+....3....+....4....+....5....+....6....+....7....+....8
A              R FORMAT1
A                CUSNBR        7S 0  10 10
A                CUSNAM        35A   10 20NOCCSID
```

OPENPRT (Open Printer File)

Level	Conditioning	Parameters
File	No	None

This keyword specifies that once a printer file is opened by the print key, it is to remain open until the display file is closed.

```
....1....+....2....+....3....+....4....+....5....+....6....+....7....+....8
A                                        PRINT(QSYSPRT)
A                                        OPENPRT
A              R FORMAT1
```

OVERLAY (Overlay)

Level	Conditioning	Parameters
Record	Yes	None

This keyword lets the current record format overlay the current screen image without necessarily clearing the screen of data. The data on the screen is not cleared as long as the record format(s) on the screen and the current record format do not overlap each other.

```
....1....+....2....+....3....+....4....+....5....+....6....+....7....+....8
A              R FORMAT1
A                                            OVERLAY
A                CUSNBR        7S 0  10 10
A                CUSNAM        35A   10 20
```

OVRATR (Override Attribute)

Level	Conditioning	Parameters
Record	Yes	None
Field		

You use this keyword with the PUTOVR keyword to send new display attributes to the screen for the specified field or record format.

```
....1....+....2....+....3....+....4....+....5....+....6....+....7....+....8
A              R FORMAT1
A   40                                        PUTOVR
A                CUSNBR        7S 0  10 100VRATR
A   42                                        DSPATR(HI)
A                CUSNAM        35A   10 20
```

OVRDTA (Override Data)

Level	Conditioning	Parameters
Record	Yes	None
Field		

You use this keyword with the PUTOVR keyword to send the data contents of a field or record format to the screen.

```
....1....+....2....+....3....+....4....+....5....+....6....+....7....+....8
A          R FORMAT1
A  40                                        PUTOVR
A            CUSNBR       7S 0   10 10
A            CUSNAM       35A    10 20OVRDTA
```

PAGEDOWN (Page Down)

Level	Conditioning	Parameters
File	Yes	1) Response indicator (optional)
Record		2) Text (optional)

Use this keyword to inform your HLL program the user has pressed the Page down or Roll up key. This keyword acts like a command function key in that all screen validity checking is performed. The PAGEDOWN keyword is the equivalent of the ROLLUP keyword.

PARAMETER DEFINITIONS

Response indicator
This optional parameter specifies the indicator to be turned on when the user presses Page down or Roll up. The valid values are 01 to 99.

Text
The text parameter contains up to 50 characters of text to serve as documentation for the keyword. You code the text within apostrophes (').

```
....1....+....2....+....3....+....4....+....5....+....6....+....7....+....8
A          R FORMAT1
A  40                                    PAGEDOWN(25 'Page Down Request')
A            CUSNBR       7S 0   10 10
A            CUSNAM       35A    10 20
```

PAGEUP (Page Up)

Level	Conditioning	Parameters
File	Yes	1) Response indicator (optional)
Record		2) Text (optional)

This keyword informs your HLL program when the user presses the Page up or Roll down key. The PAGEUP keyword acts like a command function key in that all screen validity checking is performed. This keyword is the same as the ROLLDOWN keyword.

PARAMETER DEFINITIONS

Response indicator
This optional parameter specifies the indicator to be turned on when the user presses Page up or Roll down. The valid values are 01 to 99.

Text
The text parameter contains up to 50 characters of text to serve as documentation for the keyword. You code the text within apostrophes (').

```
....1....+....2....+....3....+....4....+....5....+....6....+....7....+....8
A                    R FORMAT1
A   40                                      PAGEUP(26 'Page Up Request')
A                      CUSNBR        7S 0  10 10
A                      CUSNAM       35A     10 20
```

PASSRCD (Passed Record)

Level	Conditioning	Parameters
File	No	1) Record format

This keyword specifies that unformatted data is being passed to your program. The PASSRCD keyword works only when the first I/O operation after the display file is opened is a read request (no write) without a record format name.

PARAMETER DEFINITION

Record format
This parameter is the name of the record format that maps the data being passed to your HLL program. The record format must be in the same display file.

```
....1....+....2....+....3....+....4....+....5....+....6....+....7....+....8
A                                           PASSRCD(FORMAT1)
A                    R FORMAT1
A                      CUSNBR        7S 0  10 10
A                      CUSNAM       35A     10 20
```

PRINT (Print)

Level	Conditioning	Parameters
File	Yes	NOTE: There are two methods
Record		of defining this keyword.
		Program Control:
		1) Response indicator (optional)
		2) Text (optional)
		Printer File Control:
		1) Printer file (optional)

This keyword lets the user press the Print key to print the current display. You can specify either that an image of the screen be printed to a printer file or that control be returned to the HLL program when the user presses Print.

If you specify a response indicator or a special value of *PGM, control is returned to the program. Otherwise, the Print key prints an image of the screen to a printer file.

PARAMETER DEFINITIONS: PROGRAM CONTROL

Response indicator

This parameter is a number from 01 to 99 that corresponds to the indicator to be turned on when the user presses Print. Alternatively, you can use a special value of *PGM to indicate that control is to be returned to the HLL program.

Text

The text parameter contains up to 50 characters of text to serve as documentation for the keyword. You code the text within apostrophes (').

PARAMETER DEFINITION: PRINTER FILE CONTROL

Printer file

This optional parameter lets you indicate which printer file is to be used for output. The default is the printer file defined by the device description.

```
....1....+....2....+....3....+....4....+....5....+....6....+....7....+....8
A                                             PRINT
A          R FORMAT1

A          R FORMAT1
A   40                                        PRINT(28 'Print Function')

A          R FORMAT1
A   40                                        PRINT(*PGM)
```

PROTECT (Protect)

Level	Conditioning	Parameters
Record	Yes	None

You use this keyword with the OVERLAY keyword to protect all input-capable fields already on the screen. This keyword does not affect the input-capable fields for the record format.

```
....1....+....2....+....3....+....4....+....5....+....6....+....7....+....8
A                 R FORMAT1                   OVERLAY
A    40                                       PROTECT
A                   CUSNBR        7S 0B 10 10
A                   CUSNAM       35A  B 10 20
```

PSHBTNCHC (Push Button Choice)

Level	Conditioning	Parameters
Field	Yes	1) Choice number
		2) Choice text
		3) Command key (optional)
		4) Spacing (optional)

This keyword specifies the choices available for a push-button field (see the PSHBTNFLD keyword).

PARAMETER DEFINITIONS

Choice number
This parameter is a number from 01 to 99. Each choice must have a unique number assigned.

Choice text
This parameter is the text to be shown for the choice. You can either hard-code the parameter in the DDS or use a variable field. If you use a variable field, it must be defined in the same record format and have a data type of A and a usage of P.

You can also specify a mnemonic for the choice by placing a > character before the character to act as the mnemonic. That character appears on the screen underlined.

Command key
This optional parameter specifies the command key to be invoked when the user selects this choice. The following table lists the valid values and their meanings.

Code	Meaning
CA01-CA24	Command attention keys 1-24
CF01-CF24	Command function keys 1-24
ENTER	Enter key
HELP	Help key
HOME	Home key
PRINT	Print key
CLEAR	Clear key
ROLLUP	Roll-up request
ROLLDOWN	Roll-down request

The default for this parameter is the Enter key.

Spacing
This optional parameter indicates that a blank line is to be inserted before showing the choice. The value is *SPACEB.

```
....1....+....2....+....3....+....4....+....5....+....6....+....7....+....8
A           R FORMAT1
A             FIELD1        2Y 0B  1  2PSHBTNFLD
A                                     PSHBTNCHC(1 '>Exit' CA03)
A                                     PSHBTNCHC(2 '>Help')
A                                     PSHBTNCHC(3 '>Cancel')
A                                     PSHBTNCHC(5 &TEXT *SPACEB)
A             TEXT         10A  P
```

PSHBTNFLD (Push Button Field)

Level	Conditioning	Parameters
Field	No	1) Restrict cursor (optional)
		2) Column row (optional)
		3) Gutter (optional)

This keyword specifies a push-button field. The field for which you code the keyword must be defined with a data type of Y, be two digits long with zero decimal positions, and have a usage of I or B.

PARAMETER DEFINITIONS

Restrict cursor
This optional parameter indicates whether you want the user to be able to move the cursor outside of the push-button area. The valid values are *NORSTCSR and *RSTCSR. *NORSTCSR is the default and indicates no restriction on the cursor. *RSTCSR restricts the cursor to the push-button area.

Column row

This optional parameter determines whether the choices are displayed in multiple columns or multiple rows. The format of the parameter is either (*NUMCOL number) or (*NUMROW number), where *number* is the number of columns or rows to be used, respectively.

Displaying the choices in multiple columns causes the choices to appear in left-to-right, top-to-bottom order:

choice1 choice2 choice3
choice4 choice5 choice6

*NUMROW indicates the number of rows the push-button field should contain. All specified choices must fit on the display when placed in the specified number of rows.

Displaying the choices in multiple rows causes the choices to appear from top to bottom, then left to right, in multiple columns:

choice1 choice3 choice5
choice2 choice4 choice6

Gutter

The Gutter parameter defines the number of blanks to be used between each choice. The format of this parameter is (*GUTTER number). The number entered must be greater than one. The default gutter space is three.

```
....1....+....2....+....3....+....4....+....5....+....6....+....7....+....8
A             R FORMAT1
A               FIELD1        2Y 0B 23  2PSHBTNFLD
A                                       PSHBTNCHC(1 '>Exit')
A                                       PSHBTNCHC(2 '>Help')
A                                       PSHBTNCHC(3 '>Cancel')
A    41         FIELD2        2Y 0B 10  2PSHBTNFLD(*RSTCSR (*NUMCOL 3) +
A                                       (*GUTTER 5))
A                                       PSHBTNCHC(1 'Option #1')
A                                       PSHBTNCHC(2 'Option #2')
A                                       PSHBTNCHC(3 'Option #3')
```

PULLDOWN (Pull Down Menu)

Level	Conditioning	Parameters
Record	No	1) Selection indicator (optional)
		2) Restrict cursor (optional)

This keyword defines a record format as a pull-down menu.

PARAMETER DEFINITIONS

Selection indicator

This optional parameter specifies whether the selection indicators (i.e., radio buttons) should be displayed. The valid values are *SLTIND (to show the indicators) and *NOSLTIND (not to show them). The default is *SLTIND.

Restrict cursor

This optional parameter indicates whether to restrict the user from performing functions when the cursor is outside of the pull-down menu area. The values are *RSTCSR and *NORSTCSR. *RSTCSR prevents the user from executing pull-down menu functions when the cursor is outside the pull-down area. *NORSTCSR, the default, lets the user perform pull-down menu functions even when the cursor is outside the area.

```
....1....+....2....+....3....+....4....+....5....+....6....+....7....+....8
A          R FORMAT1                       PULLDOWN
```

PUTOVR (Put Override)

Level	Conditioning	Parameters
Record	Yes	None

PUTOVR lets you send only data or display attributes to the screen on all writes of the record format after the first write of the format. The PUTOVR keyword works with the OVRATR and OVRDTA keywords.

```
....1....+....2....+....3....+....4....+....5....+....6....+....7....+....8
A          R FORMAT1
A   40                                      PUTOVR
A            CUSNBR         7S 0B 10 100VRDTA
A            CUSNAM        35A  B 10 200VRDTA
```

PUTRETAIN (Put Retain)

Level	Conditioning	Parameters
Record	Yes	None
Field		

You use this keyword with the OVERLAY keyword to prevent data on the screen from being deleted when a record format is displayed on the screen for a second time. This keyword is similar in function to the PUTOVR keyword. PUTRETAIN is basically an older and less effective implementation of the PUTOVR keyword.

```
....1....+....2....+....3....+....4....+....5....+....6....+....7....+....8
A          R FORMAT1
A                                    PUTRETAIN   OVERLAY
```

RANGE (Range)

Level	Conditioning	Parameters
Field	No	1) Low value
		2) High value

This keyword specifies a range of valid values for an input-capable field.

PARAMETER DEFINITIONS

Low value
This parameter is the lower range of the valid values allowed for the field. This value is inclusive in the test.

High value
This parameter is the upper range of the valid values allowed for the field. This value is inclusive in the test.

```
....1....+....2....+....3....+....4....+....5....+....6....+....7....+....8
A          R FORMAT1
A            FIELD1        2Y ØB 10 10RANGE(1 15)
```

REF (Reference)

Level	Conditioning	Parameters
File	No	1) File name
		2) Record format name (optional)

This keyword specifies the name of a file from which all field references are to be retrieved. A field is referenced when an R is coded in column 29.

PARAMETER DEFINITIONS

File name
This parameter is the name of the file from which references can be retrieved. You can include the library name to qualify the file name if you wish.

Record format name
This optional parameter specifies the particular record format from the file to use for field references.

```
....1....+....2....+....3....+....4....+....5....+....6....+....7....+....8
A                                            REF(REFFILE)
A          R FORMAT1
A            CUSNBR    R            10 10
A            CUSNAM    R            10 20
A            CUSAD1          35A    11 20
....1....+....2....+....3....+....4....+....5....+....6....+....7....+....8
A                                            REF(PRODLIB/REFFILE REFFMT1)
A          R FORMAT1
A            CUSNBR    R            10 10
A            CUSNAM    R            10 20
A            CUSAD1          35A    11 20
```

REFFLD (Referenced Field)

Level	Conditioning	Parameters
Field	No	1) Field name
		2) File name (optional)

This keyword retrieves the field reference from a field in a file other than the file specified in the REF keyword.

PARAMETER DEFINITIONS

Field name

This parameter is the name of the field to reference in the other file. When the file specified has more than one record format, you can specify the name of the record format name in which the field is found.

File name

This parameter is the name of the file from which the field reference is to be retrieved. You can specify either the file name or the default value of *SRC, indicating that the field reference is in the same DDS source. You can also specify the library containing the file if you wish.

```
....1....+....2....+....3....+....4....+....5....+....6....+....7....+....8
A                                            REF(REFFILE)
A          R FORMAT1
A            PART#     R            10 10
A            ITEM            10A    11 10
A            ITEM1     R            12 10REFFLD(ITEM)
A            ITEM2     R            13 10REFFLD(FORMAT1/ITEM)
A            ITEM3     R            14 10REFFLD(ITEM *SRC)
A            ITEM4     R            15 10REFFLD(ITEM FILE2)
A            ITEM5     R            16 10REFFLD(ITEM PRODLIB/FILE2)
```

RETCMDKEY (Retain Command Key)

Level	Conditioning	Parameters
Record	No	None

This keyword retains as active all command keys already active on the screen when the record format is written to the screen. RETCMDKEY is used mainly with System/36 Environment applications.

This keyword affects CA01-CA24 and CF01-CF24 definitions.

```
....1....+....2....+....3....+....4....+....5....+....6....+....7....+....8
A           R FORMAT1                   CF12

A           R FORMAT2
A                                       RETCMDKEY
A                                       OVERLAY
```

RETKEY (Retain Function Key)

Level	Conditioning	Parameters
Record	No	None

This keyword retains as active all function keys already active on the screen when the record format is written. The RETKEY keyword is used mainly with System/36 Environment applications.

The functions retained by this keyword are CLEAR, HELP, HLPRTN, HOME, PAGEDOWN, PAGEUP, ROLLDOWN, and ROLLUP.

```
....1....+....2....+....3....+....4....+....5....+....6....+....7....+....8
A           R FORMAT1                   PAGEUP

A           R FORMAT2
A                                       RETKEY
A                                       OVERLAY
```

RETLCKSTS (Retain Lock Status)

Level	Conditioning	Parameters
Record	Yes	None

This keyword retains the keyboard's locked status on the next input operation of the record format.

```
....1....+....2....+....3....+....4....+....5....+....6....+....7....+....8
A           R FORMAT1
A    40                                 RETLCKSTS
A             CUSNBR          7S 0B 10 10
A             CUSNAM         35A  B 10 20
```

RMVWDW (Remove Window)

Level	Conditioning	Parameters
Record	Yes	None

This keyword removes all active windows from the screen before the current window is sent.

```
....1....+....2....+....3....+....4....+....5....+....6....+....7....+....8
A                      R FORMAT1                        WINDOW(10 10  5  50)
A    40                                                 RMVWDW
A                        CUSNBR        7S 0    2  2
A                        CUSNAM       35A      2 10
```

ROLLDOWN (Roll Down)

Level	Conditioning	Parameters
File	Yes	1) Response indicator (optional)
Record		2) Text (optional)

This keyword informs your HLL program when the user has pressed the Roll down or Page up key. The ROLLDOWN keyword acts like a command function key in that all screen validity checking is performed. This keyword is the equivalent of the PAGEUP keyword.

PARAMETER DEFINITIONS

Response indicator
This optional parameter specifies the indicator number to be turned on when the user presses the Roll down or Page up key. The valid values are 01 to 99.

Text
The text parameter contains up to 50 characters of text to serve as documentation for the keyword. You code the text within apostrophes (').

```
....1....+....2....+....3....+....4....+....5....+....6....+....7....+....8
A                      R FORMAT1
A    40                                      ROLLDOWN(25 'Roll Down Request')
A                        CUSNBR        7S 0   10 10
A                        CUSNAM       35A     10 20
```

ROLLUP (Roll Up)

Level	Conditioning	Parameters
File	Yes	1) Response indicator (optional)
Record		2) Text (optional)

This keyword informs your HLL program when the user has pressed the Roll up or Page down key. The ROLLUP keyword acts like a command function key in that all screen validity checking is performed. This keyword is the same as the PAGEDOWN keyword.

PARAMETER DEFINITIONS

Response indicator
This optional parameter specifies the indicator to be turned on when the user presses Roll up or Page down. The valid values are 01 to 99.

Text
The text parameter contains up to 50 characters of text to serve as documentation for the keyword. You code the text within apostrophes (').

```
....1....+....2....+....3....+....4....+....5....+....6....+....7....+....8
A              R FORMAT1
A   40                                   ROLLUP(26 'Roll Up Request')
A                 CUSNBR       7S 0  10 10
A                 CUSNAM      35A      10 20
```

RTNCSRLOC (Return Cursor Location)

Level	Conditioning	Parameters
Record	No	NOTE: There are two formats for this keyword.
		Record Format:
		1) Return qualifier (optional)
		2) Cursor record
		3) Cursor field
		4) Cursor position (optional)
		Window/Mouse Format:
		1) Return qualifier
		2) Cursor row
		3) Cursor column
		4) Cursor row 2 (optional)
		5) Cursor column 2 (optional)

This keyword returns the location of the cursor on the screen. Which of the two keyword formats you use depends on the type of cursor location you're requesting. The first format returns the location within a record format on the screen. The second format returns the location within a window or from a pointer device, such as a mouse.

PARAMETER DEFINITIONS: RECORD FORMAT

Return qualifier

This optional parameter returns the location for a record format. The value is *RECNAME.

Cursor record

This parameter is the name of the field that returns the name of the record format in which the cursor is located. The field must be defined in the same record format, have a data type of A, be 10 characters long, and have a usage of H.

Cursor field

This parameter specifies the field that returns the name of the field in which the cursor is located. The field must be defined in the same record format, have a data type of A, be 10 characters long, and have a usage of H.

Cursor position

This optional parameter specifies a field that returns to your program the relative location of the cursor in a field. The field must be defined in the same record format, have a data type of S, be four digits long with zero decimal positions, and have a usage of H.

WINDOW/MOUSE FORMAT

Return qualifier

This required parameter indicates whether you want to return the cursor from a window or a mouse. The valid values are *WINDOW and *MOUSE.

Cursor row

This parameter specifies a field that returns the row of the cursor on the screen. The field must be defined within the same record format, have a data type of S, be three digits long with zero decimal positions, and have a usage of H.

Cursor column

This parameter is the name of a field that returns the column of the cursor on the screen. The field must be defined within the same record format, have a data type of S, be three digits long with zero decimal positions, and have a usage of H.

Cursor row 2

This optional parameter specifies a field to return the row of the cursor relative to either the current active window (when the return qualifier parameter is *WINDOW) or the row of the cursor before the start of a two-event mouse definition (when the return qualifier parameter is *MOUSE). The field must be defined in the same record format, have a data type of S, be three digits long with zero decimal positions, and have a usage of H.

Cursor column 2

This optional parameter is the name of a field that returns either the column of the cursor relative to the current active window (when the return qualifier parameter is *WINDOW) or the row of the cursor before the start of a two-event mouse definition (when the return qualifier parameter is *MOUSE). The field must be defined within the same record format, have a data type of S, be three digits long with zero decimal positions, and have a usage of H.

```
....1....+....2....+....3....+....4....+....5....+....6....+....7....+....8
A           R FORMAT1                    RTNCSRLOC(&RCD &FIELD &POS)
A                                        RTNCSRLOC(*MOUSE &ROW &COL   +
A                                        &ROW2 &COL2)
A             RCD        10A   H
A             FIELD      10A   H
A             POS         4S  0H
A             ROW         3S  0H
A             COL         3S  0H
A             ROW2        3S  0H
A             COL2        3S  0H

A           R FORMAT2                    WINDOW(10 10  5 50)
A                                        RTNCSRLOC(*WINDOW &ROW &COL)
A             ROW         3S  0H
A             COL         3S  0H
```

RTNDTA (Return Data)

Level	Conditioning	Parameters
Record	No	None

This keyword lets your HLL program perform a second read (READ opcode in RPG) of the record format without having to resend the record format to the screen. The second read returns the same data received on the first read of the record format.

```
....1....+....2....+....3....+....4....+....5....+....6....+....7....+....8
A           R FORMAT1
A                                        RTNDTA
A             CUSNBR      7S  0B 10 10
A             CUSNAM     35A   B 10 20
```

SETOF (Set Off)

Level	Conditioning	Parameters
Record	No	1) Response indicator
		2) Text (optional)

This keyword turns off an indicator when control is returned to your HLL program.

PARAMETER DEFINITIONS

Response indicator

This parameter contains a numeral from 01 to 99 indicating the indicator to be turned off.

Text

The text parameter contains up to 50 characters of text to serve as documentation for the keyword. You code the text within apostrophes (').

```
....1....+....2....+....3....+....4....+....5....+....6....+....7....+....8
A            R FORMAT1                         SETOF(40 'Turn off alarm')
A    40                                        ALARM
A              CUSNBR          7S 0   10 10
A              CUSNAM         35A     10 20
```

SETOFF (Set Off)

Level	Conditioning	Parameters
Record	No	1) Response indicator
		2) Text (optional)

This keyword is the same as the SETOF keyword, but SETOF is preferred.

SFL (Subfile)

Level	Conditioning	Parameters
Record	No	None

This keyword specifies a record format as a subfile record format.

```
....1....+....2....+....3....+....4....+....5....+....6....+....7....+....8
A            R SFLFMT1                 SFL
A              OPTION          1A      5 2
A              OPTTXT         20A      5 5
```

SFLCHCCTL (Subfile Choice Control)

Level	Conditioning	Parameters
Field	No	1) Message ID (optional)
		2) Message file (optional)

This keyword defines a subfile as a selection-list subfile. The field that contains the keyword must be the first field defined in the subfile record format.

The field acts as the control field for the selection list. The field must be defined with a data type of Y, be one digit long with zero decimal positions, and have a usage of H.

The values sent from and to your HLL program control the availability of the choices in the selection list. The table below shows the values you can use with this control field.

Value	Meaning on Output	Meaning on Input
0	Available	Not selected by user
1	Set as default	Selected by user
2	Unavailable — user cannot place cursor on this choice unless help has been defined	
3	Unavailable — user cannot place cursor on this choice	
4	Unavailable — user cannot place cursor on this choice	

PARAMETER DEFINITIONS

Message ID

This optional parameter lets you specify the message to be displayed when the user selects a choice that is not available. You can either specify this value in the DDS or use a variable field. If you use a variable field, it must be defined within the same record format, have a data type of A, be seven characters long, and have a usage of P.

Message file

This optional parameter is required when you specify Message ID. This parameter specifies the name of the message file in which the message ID is located. You can qualify the name of the file with the library name if you wish. You can either hard-code the message file or use a variable field. If you use a variable field for the file or library, it must be defined within the same record format, have a data type of A, be ten characters long, and have a usage of P.

```
....1....+....2....+....3....+....4....+....5....+....6....+....7....+....8
A           R SFLFMT1                    SFL
A             FIELD1         1Y 0H       SFLCHCCTL(USR0025 USERMSGF)
A             CHCTXT        10A      5 10
```

SFLCLR (Subfile Clear)

Level	Conditioning	Parameters
Record	Yes	None

This keyword clears the contents of a subfile when a write is issued to the subfile-control format and the keyword is active. The SFLCLR keyword is valid only in the subfile-control record format.

```
....1....+....2....+....3....+....4....+....5....+....6....+....7....+....8
A             R SFLCTL1                      SFLCTL(SFLFMT1)
A   40                                       SFLCLR
A  N40                                       SFLDSPCTL
A  N40                                       SFLDSP
```

SFLCSRPRG (Subfile Cursor Progression)

Level	Conditioning	Parameters
Field	No	None

This keyword causes the cursor, when moved out of the field, to be positioned to the same field in the next subfile record. The SFLCSRPRG keyword is valid only in the subfile record format.

```
....1....+....2....+....3....+....4....+....5....+....6....+....7....+....8
A             R SSFLFMT1                      SFL
A               FIELD1        2A  B   5   4SFLCSRPRG
A               FIELD2       10A  B   5  10
```

SFLCSRRRN (Subfile Cursor Relative Record Number)

Level	Conditioning	Parameters
Record	No	1) Relative record

This keyword returns the relative record number of the subfile record on which the cursor is located when control is returned to your HLL program. The SFLCSRRRN keyword is used in the subfile-control record format.

PARAMETER DEFINITION

Relative record

This parameter is the name of a field that contains the relative record number. The field must be defined in the same record format, have a data type of S, be five digits long with zero decimal positions, and have a usage of H.

```
....1....+....2....+....3....+....4....+....5....+....6....+....7....+....8
A             R SFLCTL1                      SFLCTL(SFLFMT1)
A                                            SFLCSRRRN(&RRN)
A               RRN          5S  0H
```

SFLCTL (Subfile Control)

Level	Conditioning	Parameters
Record	No	1) Subfile name

This keyword defines a record format as a subfile-control record format and links the control format to the subfile record format defined by the SFL keyword. The subfile record format must be defined before the subfile-control record format.

PARAMETER DEFINITION

Subfile name
This parameter is the name of the subfile record format.

```
....1....+....2....+....3....+....4....+....5....+....6....+....7....+....8
A          R SFLFMT1               SFL
   .
   .
   .
A          R SFLCTL1               SFLCTL(SFLFMT1)
```

SFLDLT (Subfile Delete)

Level	Conditioning	Parameters
Record	Yes	None

This keyword deletes a subfile. You use the SFLDLT keyword mainly when you need to display another subfile when the maximum number of subfiles (12) are already active. In this case, you must delete an active subfile before building the new subfile. You can specify this keyword only in the subfile-control record format.

```
....1....+....2....+....3....+....4....+....5....+....6....+....7....+....8
A          R SFLCTL1               SFLCTL(SFLFMT1)
A   40                             SFLDLT
```

SFLDROP (Subfile Drop)

Level	Conditioning	Parameters
Record	Yes	1) Command key

This keyword defines a command key to be used to fold or truncate a subfile when it occupies more than one line on the screen. The SFLDROP keyword is valid only in the subfile-control record format. The subfile is displayed in truncated mode as the default (see also SFLFOLD and SFLMODE).

PARAMETER DEFINITION

Command key

This parameter is the command key the user must press to switch the mode in which the subfile is displayed. The valid values are CA*nn* or CF*nn*, where *nn* is a number from 01 to 24.

```
....1....+....2....+....3....+....4....+....5....+....6....+....7....+....8
A              R SFLFMT1                        SFL
A                FIELD1          1A  B  5  2
A                FIELD2         30A  0  6  2
A              R SFLCTL1                         SFLCTL(SFLFMT1)
A    40                                          SFLDROP(CA07)
```

SFLDSP (Subfile Display)

Level	Conditioning	Parameters
Record	Yes	None

This keyword indicates when the subfile record contents are to be displayed on the screen. The SFLDSP keyword is valid only in the subfile-control record format.
   The subfile cannot be empty when it's displayed.

```
....1....+....2....+....3....+....4....+....5....+....6....+....7....+....8
A              R SFLCTL1                         SFLCTL(SFLFMT1)
A    40                                          SFLDSP
```

SFLDSPCTL (Subfile Display Control)

Level	Conditioning	Parameters
Record	Yes	None

This keyword indicates when the subfile-control record format contents are to be displayed on the screen. The SFLDSPCTL keyword is valid only in the subfile-control record format.

```
....1....+....2....+....3....+....4....+....5....+....6....+....7....+....8
A              R SFLCTL1                         SFLCTL(SFLFMT1)
A    40                                          SFLDSPCTL
A                CUSNBR          7S  0B 10 10
A                CUSNAM         35A  B  10 20
```

SFLEND (Subfile End)

Level	Conditioning	Parameters
Record	Yes	1) More indicator (optional)
		2) Scroll indicator (optional)

This keyword defines what indication is given to the user when more than one subfile page of data is available. You must use a conditioning indicator with this keyword. When the conditioning test is true, the last page of the subfile indicates there are no more records to be displayed. When the conditioning test is false, the last page of the loaded subfile indicates that more records exist even though the last page of data has been displayed.

PARAMETER DEFINITIONS

More indicator

This optional parameter specifies what type of symbol is used to indicate the availability of additional subfile information. The valid values are *PLUS (the default), *MORE, and *SCRBAR.

*PLUS specifies that a plus sign (+) is used to indicate that more data exists. The last page will not show a plus sign.

*MORE specifies that the text "More..." or "Bottom" is used below the last line occupied by the subfile to indicate that more data exists or that there is no more data, respectively.

*SCRBAR specifies that a graphical scroll bar is used to indicate the position of the displayed data in the subfile.

Scroll indicator

You use this optional parameter only when you've specified *SCRBAR in the first parameter. The scroll indicator defines how the scroll bar is to appear when the display does not support graphical presentations. The valid values are *SCRBAR, *MORE, and *PLUS. The default is *SCRBAR.

*SCRBAR indicates that a text-based image of a scroll bar is to be presented.

*MORE indicates that the text "More..." and "Bottom" is to be used, just as if you had specified *MORE for the more indicator.

*PLUS indicates that a plus sign (+) is to be used, just as if you had specified *PLUS rather than *SCRBAR.

```
....1....+....2....+....3....+....4....+....5....+....6....+....7....+....8
A           R SFLCTL1               SFLCTL(SFLFMT1)
A   40                              SFLEND(*MORE)
```

SFLENTER (Subfile Enter)

Level	Conditioning	Parameters
Record	No	1) Command key

This keyword is used to specify that the Enter key is to act like the Page up key. The command key defined by this keyword acts like the Enter key. The SFLENTER keyword is valid only on the subfile control record format.

PARAMETER DEFINITION

Command key

This parameter specifies a command key that, when pressed, acts like a normal Enter key and returns control to the HLL program. The valid values are CA01-CA24 and CF01-CF24.

```
....1....+....2....+....3....+....4....+....5....+....6....+....7....+....8
A          R SFLCTL1                      SFLCTL(SFLFMT1)
A                                         SFLENTER(CF07)
```

SFLFOLD (Subfile Fold)

Level	Conditioning	Parameters
Record	Yes	1) Command key

This keyword defines a command key to be used to fold or truncate a subfile when it occupies more than one line on the screen. The SFLFOLD keyword is valid only in the subfile-control record format. The subfile is displayed in the folded mode when this keyword is used (see also SFLDROP and SFLMODE).

PARAMETER DEFINITION

Command key

This parameter specifies the command key the user must press to switch the subfile display mode between folded and truncated. The valid values are CAnn or CFnn, where nn is a number from 01 to 24.

```
....1....+....2....+....3....+....4....+....5....+....6....+....7....+....8
A          R SFLFMT1                      SFL
A            FIELD1          1A  B  5  2
A            FIELD2         30A  0  6  2
A          R SFLCTL1                      SFLCTL(SFLFMT1)
A   40                                    SFLFOLD(CA07)
```

SFLINZ (Subfile Initialize)

Level	Conditioning	Parameters
Record	Yes	None

This keyword initializes the contents of each subfile record to blanks or zeros on an output operation to the subfile-control record format (see also SFLRNA).

```
....1....+....2....+....3....+....4....+....5....+....6....+....7....+....8
A          R SFLCTL1                      SFLCTL(SFLFMT1)
A   40                                    SFLINZ
```

SFLLIN (Subfile Line)

Level	Conditioning	Parameters
Record	No	1) Spaces

This keyword displays a subfile horizontally (that is, in multiple columns across the screen). The SFLLIN keyword is valid only on the subfile-control record format.

PARAMETER DEFINITION

Spaces
This parameter specifies the number of spaces used between subfile columns.

```
....1....+....2....+....3....+....4....+....5....+....6....+....7....+....8
A          R SFLCTL1                    SFLCTL(SFLFMT1)
A                                       SFLLIN(3)
```

SFLMLTCHC (Subfile Multiple Choice Selection List)

Level	Conditioning	Parameters
Record	No	1) Number selected (optional)
		2) Restrict cursor (optional)
		3) Selection indicator (optional)

This keyword defines a subfile selection list as a multiple-choice list. The SFLMLTCHC keyword is valid only in the subfile-control record format.

PARAMETER DEFINITIONS

Number selected
This optional parameter is a field that contains the number of choices the user makes. This field must be defined in the same record format, have a data type of Y, be four digits long with zero decimal positions, and have a usage of H.

Restrict cursor
This optional parameter indicates whether to restrict the user from moving the cursor outside the choice area defined by the subfile. The values are *RSTCSR and *NORSTCSR. *RSTCSR prevents the user from moving the cursor outside the choice area. *NORSTCSR is the default and lets the user move the cursor outside the area.

Selection indicator
This optional parameter indicates whether the selection indicators (i.e., check boxes) should be displayed. The valid values are *SLTIND and *NOSLTIND. *SLTIND shows the selection indicators; *NOSLTIND does not. The default is *NOSLTIND.

```
....1....+....2....+....3....+....4....+....5....+....6....+....7....+....8
A          R SFLFMT1                         SFL
A            FIELD1          1Y ØH           SFLCHCCTL
A            CHCTXT         1ØA  O   5 1Ø
A          R SFLCTL1                         SFLCTL(SFLFMT1)
A                                            SFLMLTCHC(&NBR *RSTCSR *SLTIND)
A            NBR             4Y ØH
```

SFLMODE (Subfile Mode)

Level	Conditioning	Parameters
Record	No	1) Mode

This keyword returns to your HLL program the current mode (either truncated or folded) of a multiple-line subfile. SFLMODE is valid only in the subfile-control record format (see also SFLDROP and SFLFOLD).

PARAMETER DEFINITION

Mode

This parameter is the name of a field that contains the subfile's mode. The value returned is either a 0 (for folded mode) or a 1 (for truncated mode). The field must be defined in the same record format, have a data type of A, be one character long, and have a usage of H.

```
....1....+....2....+....3....+....4....+....5....+....6....+....7....+....8
A          R SFLCTL1                         SFLCTL(SFLFMT1)
A                                            SFLMODE(&MODE)
A   4Ø                                       SFLDROP(CFØ7)
A   41                                       SFLFOLD(CFØ7)
A            MODE            1A  H
```

SFLMSG (Subfile Message)

Level	Conditioning	Parameters
Record	Yes	1) Message text
		2) Response indicator (optional)

This keyword displays a message for a subfile. The keyword acts like an error message but is not associated with a specific field. The SFLMSG keyword is valid only in the subfile control record format.

PARAMETER DEFINITIONS

Message text

This parameter is the error message to be displayed. The message can contain as much text as will fit in the screen. The text is entered within apostrophes (').

Response indicator
This optional parameter turns a specific indicator off when control is returned to the HLL program. The indicator used is normally the same one specified in the conditioning columns.

```
....1....+....2....+....3....+....4....+....5....+....6....+....7....+....8
A               R SFLCTL1                  SFLCTL(SFLFMT1)
A   70                                     SFLMSG('Invalid customer #')
A   71                                     SFLMSG('Name cannot be blank' 71)
```

SFLMSGID (Subfile Message Identifier)

Level	Conditioning	Parameters
Record	Yes	1) Message ID
		2) Message file
		3) Response indicator (optional)
		4) Message data (optional)

This keyword displays a message from a message file for a subfile. The SFLMSGID keyword acts like the ERRMSGID keyword but is not associated with a specific field. SFLMSGID is valid only in the subfile control record format.

PARAMETER DEFINITIONS

Message ID
This parameter is the seven-character identifier of the message to be displayed.

Message file
This parameter is the name of the message file that contains the message ID. You can qualify the file name with the name of the library if you wish.

Response indicator
This optional parameter turns a specific indicator off when control is returned to your HLL program. The indicator is normally the same one specified in the conditioning columns.

Message data
You use this optional parameter to pass data from your HLL program to the message identifier. The field name must be defined in the same record format, have a data type of A, and have a usage of P. The length of the field depends on the message ID requirements.

```
....1....+....2....+....3....+....4....+....5....+....6....+....7....+....8
A           R SFLCTL1                     SFLCTL(SFLFMT1)
A    70                                   SFLMSGID(USR0020 USERMSGF)
A    71                                   SFLMSGID(USR0021 PRODLIB/USERMSGF +
A                                         71 &DATA)
A           DATA          10A   P
```

SFLMSGKEY (Subfile Message Key)

Level	Conditioning	Parameters
Field	No	None

This keyword specifies the messages to be loaded in a message subfile. SFLMSGKEY is used in the subfile record format and is placed on the first field defined in the message subfile (see also SFLMSGRCD and SFLPGMQ).

```
....1....+....2....+....3....+....4....+....5....+....6....+....7....+....8
A           R SFLMSG                      SFL
A                                         SFLMSGRCD(20)
A              MSGKEY                     SFLMSGKEY
A              MSGPGM                     SFLPGMQ
A           R SFLMSGC                     SFLCTL(SFLMSG)
A    40                                   SFLINZ
A                                         SFLPAG(3)
A                                         SFLSIZ(3)
A                                         SFLDSP
A                                         SFLDSPCTL
A              MSGPGM                     SFLPGMQ
```

SFLMSGRCD (Subfile Message Record)

Level	Conditioning	Parameters
Record	No	1) Line number

This keyword defines a subfile as a message subfile. The SFLMSGRCD keyword is valid only in the subfile record format (see also SFLMSGKEY and SFLPGMQ).

PARAMETER DEFINITION

Line number
This parameter specifies the line on which the message file is to be displayed. The number must be valid for the screen size being used.

```
....1....+....2....+....3....+....4....+....5....+....6....+....7....+....8
A           R SFLMSG                      SFL
A                                         SFLMSGRCD(20)
A              MSGKEY                     SFLMSGKEY
A              MSGPGM                     SFLPGMQ
A           R SFLMSGC                     SFLCTL(SFLMSG)
A    40                                   SFLINZ
A                                         SFLPAG(3)
A                                         SFLSIZ(3)
A                                         SFLDSP
A                                         SFLDSPCTL
A              MSGPGM                     SFLPGMQ
```

SFLNXTCHG (Subfile Next Changed)

Level	Conditioning	Parameters
Record	Yes	None

This keyword tags a subfile record as being modified at the time it is written to the subfile or when your HLL program updates the subfile. The SFLNXTCHG keyword is valid only in the subfile record format.

```
....1....+....2....+....3....+....4....+....5....+....6....+....7....+....8
A              R SFLFMT1                     SFL
A    40                                      SFLNXTCHG
A                  OPTION        1A  B  5  2
A                  OPTTXT       20A     5 10
```

SFLPAG (Subfile Page)

Level	Conditioning	Parameters
Record	No	1) Number records

This keyword defines how many subfile records are to be displayed on the screen at one time (in other words, one page of data). The SFLPAG keyword is valid only in the subfile-control record format.

PARAMETER DEFINITION

Number records
This parameter contains the number of records to be displayed.

```
....1....+....2....+....3....+....4....+....5....+....6....+....7....+....8
A              R SFLCTL1                     SFLCTL(SFLFMT1)
A                                            SFLPAG(3)
```

SFLPGMQ (Subfile Program Message Queue)

Level	Conditioning	Parameters
Field	No	None

This keyword indicates that the field contains the name of the program message queue used to build a message subfile. SFLPGMQ is specified in both the subfile record format and the subfile-control record format (see also SFLMSGKEY and SFLMSGRCD).

```
....1....+....2....+....3....+....4....+....5....+....6....+....7....+....8
A            R SFLMSG                      SFL
A                                          SFLMSGRCD(20)
A              MSGKEY                       SFLMSGKEY
A              MSGPGM                       SFLPGMQ
A            R SFLMSGC                      SFLCTL(SFLMSG)
A      40                                   SFLINZ
A                                           SFLPAG(3)
A                                           SFLSIZ(3)
A                                           SFLDSP
A                                           SFLDSPCTL
A              PGMNAM                        SFLPGMQ
```

SFLRCDNBR (Subfile Record Number)

Level	Conditioning	Parameters
Field	No	1) Position

This keyword specifies the page of data to be shown to the user first when the subfile is displayed on the screen. SFLRCDNBR is used only in the subfile-control record format.

PARAMETER DEFINITION

Position

This parameter defines whether the cursor is to be placed on the record identified by the keyword or whether that record should be the first record shown on the screen. The valid values are CURSOR and *TOP. CURSOR places the cursor on the subfile record indicated by the field. *TOP displays the subfile record as the first line of the page.

```
....1....+....2....+....3....+....4....+....5....+....6....+....7....+....8
A            R SFLCTL1                     SFLCTL(SFLFMT1)
A              RRN           4S  0H         SFLRCDNBR(CURSOR)
```

SFLRNA (Subfile Record Not Active)

Level	Conditioning	Parameters
Record	No	None

This keyword specifies that records initialized by the SFLINZ keyword are not to be considered active by the display file. The SFLRNA keyword is valid only in the subfile-control record format.

```
....1....+....2....+....3....+....4....+....5....+....6....+....7....+....8
A            R SFLCTL1                     SFLCTL(SFLFMT1)
A      40                                   SFLINZ
A                                           SFLRNA
```

SFLROLVAL (Subfile Roll Value)

Level	Conditioning	Parameters
Field	No	None

This keyword specifies an input-capable field into which the user can key a value telling the system how many records to page up or down when the user makes a Roll request. The SFLROLVAL keyword is valid only in the subfile-control record format.

```
....1....+....2....+....3....+....4....+....5....+....6....+....7....+....8
A              R SFLCTL1                    SFLCTL(SFLFMT1)
A                ROLNBR         4S 0B 10 10SFLROLVAL
```

SFLRTNSEL (Subfile Return Selected Choices)

Level	Conditioning	Parameters
Record	No	None

You can use this keyword with the SFLMLTCHC and SFLSNGCHC keywords to indicate which selected records are to be returned to your program. SFLRTNSEL is used only in the subfile control record format.

If you do not use this keyword, only those choices the user specifically selects are returned to the program. Choices selected as default choices are not returned.

When you use this keyword, all choices are returned to the HLL program.

```
....1....+....2....+....3....+....4....+....5....+....6....+....7....+....8
A              R SFLCTL1                    SFLCTL(SFLFMT1)
A                                           SFLMLTCHC
A                                           SFLRTNSEL
```

SFLSCROLL (Subfile Scroll)

Level	Conditioning	Parameters
Field	No	None

This keyword returns to the HLL program the relative record number of the subfile record currently displayed at the top of the subfile. SFLSCROLL is valid only in the subfile-control record format.

The field in which this keyword is placed must be defined with a data type of S, be five digits long with zero decimal positions, and have a usage of H.

```
....1....+....2....+....3....+....4....+....5....+....6....+....7....+....8
A              R SFLCTL1                    SFLCTL(SFLFMT1)
A                PAGRRN         5S 0H       SFLSCROLL
```

SFLSIZ (Subfile Size)

Level	Conditioning	Parameters
Record	No	1) Number records

This keyword specifies the default number of records in a subfile. You can specify the SFLSIZ keyword only in the subfile control record format.

PARAMETER DEFINITION

Number records
This parameter is a number from 01 to 9999 that indicates the default number of records in the subfile. The value entered must be greater than or equal to the value specified in the SFLPAG keyword.

```
....1....+....2....+....3....+....4....+....5....+....6....+....7....+....8
A          R SFLCTL1                  SFLCTL(SFLFMT1)
A                                     SFLSIZ(30)
A                                     SFLPAG(10)
```

SFLSNGCHC (Subfile Single Choice Selection List)

Level	Conditioning	Parameters
Record	No	1) Restrict cursor (optional)
		2) Selection indicator (optional)
		3) Auto selection (optional)

This keyword defines a subfile selection list as a single-choice list. SFLSNGCHC is valid only in the subfile-control record format.

PARAMETER DEFINITIONS

Restrict cursor
This optional parameter indicates whether the user is restricted from moving the cursor outside the choice area defined by the subfile. The values are *RSTCSR and *NORSTCSR. *RSTCSR prevents the user from moving the cursor outside the choice area. *NORSTCSR is the default and lets the user move the cursor outside the choice area.

Selection indicator
This optional parameter specifies whether the selection indicators (i.e., radio buttons) should be displayed. The valid values are *SLTIND and *NOSLTIND. *SLTIND shows the selection indicators; *NOSLTIND does not. The default is *NOSLTIND.

Auto selection

This optional parameter indicates whether the Enter key automatically selects the choice on which the cursor is currently positioned. The valid values are *AUTOSLT, *AUTOSLTENH, and *NOAUTOSLT. *AUTOSLT selects the choice when Enter is pressed. *AUTOSLTENH selects the choice only when the system is running on an enhanced controller. *NOAUTOSLT does not automatically select the choice when the user presses Enter.

The default for this parameter is *AUTOSLT if the selection list is defined in a pull-down menu; otherwise, the default is *NOAUTOSLT.

```
....1....+....2....+....3....+....4....+....5....+....6....+....7....+....8
A          R SFLFMT1                   SFL
A            FIELD1        1Y 0H        SFLCHCCTL
A            CHCTXT       10A  0  5 10
A          R SFLCTL1                    SFLCTL(SFLFMT1)
A                                       SFLSNGCHC(*RSTCSR *SLTIND *AUTOSLT)
A            NBR           4Y 0H
```

SLNO (Starting Line Number)

Level	Conditioning	Parameters
Record	No	1) Line number

This keyword specifies a particular line number on which the record format is to start.

PARAMETER DEFINITION

Line number

This parameter indicates the line number on which the record format is to start. You can either hard-code a parameter value from 01 to 27, or you can use the special value *VAR. *VAR indicates that the starting location is determined by your HLL program at runtime.

```
....1....+....2....+....3....+....4....+....5....+....6....+....7....+....8
A          R FORMAT1
A                                       SLNO(*VAR)
```

SNGCHCFLD (Single Choice Field)

Level	Conditioning	Parameters
Field	No	1) Restrict cursor (optional)
		2) Selection indicator (optional)
		3) Auto selection (optional)
		4) Auto enter (optional)
		5) Column row (optional)
		6) Gutter (optional)

This keyword defines a field as a single-choice field.

PARAMETER DEFINITIONS

Restrict cursor

This optional parameter indicates whether to restrict the user from moving the cursor outside the choice area defined by the field. The values are *RSTCSR and *NORSTCSR. *RSTCSR prevents the user from moving the cursor outside the choice area; *NORSTCSR does not. *NORSTCSR is the default.

Selection indicator

This optional parameter indicates whether the selection indicators (i.e., radio buttons) should be displayed. The valid values are *SLTIND and *NOSLTIND. *SLTIND shows the selection indicators; *NOSLTIND does not. The default is *SLTIND.

Auto selection

This optional parameter indicates whether the Enter key automatically selects the choice on which the cursor is currently positioned. The valid values are *AUTOSLT, *AUTOSLTENH, and *NOAUTOSLT. *AUTOSLT selects the choice when the user presses Enter. *AUTOSLTENH selects the choice only when the system is running on an enhanced controller. *NOAUTOSLT does not automatically select the choice when the user presses Enter. The default is *AUTOSLT.

Auto enter

This optional parameter indicates whether control is returned to the HLL program as soon as a selection is made. The valid values are *AUTOENT, *NOAUTOENT, and *AUTOENTNN. *AUTOENT returns control when a selection is made as long as a double-digit selection number is not required. *NOAUTOENT does not return control when a selection is made; *NOAUTOENT is the default. *AUTOENTNN returns control only when a numeric selection is not required.

Column row

This optional parameter defines how the choices are displayed (in multiple columns or multiple rows). The format of this parameter is either (*NUMCOL number) or (*NUMROW number). Depending on the format, you enter either the number of columns or rows to be used.

Displaying the choices in multiple columns causes the choices to appear in left-to-right, top-to-bottom order:

```
choice1    choice2    choice3
choice4    choice5    choice6
```

Displaying the choices in multiple rows causes the choices to appear from top to bottom, then left to right, in multiple columns:

```
choice1    choice3    choice5
choice2    choice4    choice6
```

Gutter

If you specify *NUMCOL or *NUMROW, you can also specify this optional parameter. Gutter defines the number of blanks to be used between choices. The format of this parameter is (*GUTTER number). The number you enter must be greater than one. The default gutter space is three.

```
....1....+....2....+....3....+....4....+....5....+....6....+....7....+....8
A              FIELD1        2Y 0B  1  2SNGCHCFLD(*RSTCSR *NOSLTIND +
A                                        *AUTOSLT *AUTOENTNN   +
A                                        (*NUMCOL 3) (*GUTTER 5))
A                                        CHOICE(1 'Update')
A                                        CHOICE(2 'Add')
A                                        CHOICE(3 'Delete')
A              FIELD2        2Y 0B 10  2SNGCHCFLD
A                                        CHOICE(1 'Choice #1')
A                                        CHOICE(2 'Choice #2')
```

SYSNAME (System Name)

Level	Conditioning	Parameters
Field	No	None

This keyword displays the current system name as an output field on the screen. This field is 8 characters long.

```
....1....+....2....+....3....+....4....+....5....+....6....+....7....+....8
A              R FORMAT1
A                                      1 62'System:'
A                                      1 72SYSNAME
```

TEXT (Text)

Level	Conditioning	Parameters
Record	No	1) Description
Field		

This keyword adds descriptive text to record formats or fields. The text serves as documentation only.

PARAMETER DEFINITION

Description

This parameter is a text field up to 50 characters long enclosed in apostrophes (').

```
....1....+....2....+....3....+....4....+....5....+....6....+....7....+....8
A              R FORMAT1
A                CUSNBR        7S 0  10 10TEXT('Customer #')
A                CUSNAM       35A     10 20
```

TIME (Time)

Level	Conditioning	Parameters
Field	No	None

This keyword displays the current system time on the screen.

```
....1....+....2....+....3....+....4....+....5....+....6....+....7....+....8
A            R FORMAT1
A                                       1  2'Time:'
A                                       1  8TIME
```

TIMFMT (Time Format)

Level	Conditioning	Parameters
Field	No	1) Time format

This keyword defines the time format for a time field.

PARAMETER DEFINITION

Time format
This parameter is a code that represents the format of a time field.

Code	Meaning	Format
*HMS	Hours:minutes:seconds	hh:mm:ss
*ISO	International Standards Organization	hh.mm.ss
*USA	USA standard	hh:mm AM or hh:mm PM
*EUR	European standard	hh.mm.ss
*JIS	Japanese standard	hh:mm:ss

```
....1....+....2....+....3....+....4....+....5....+....6....+....7....+....8
A            R FORMAT1
A              TIMFLD1        T    10 10TIMFMT(*ISO)
A              TIMFLD2        T    12 10TIMFMT(*USA)
A              TIMFLD3        T    14 10TIMFMT(*HMS)
```

TIMSEP (Time Separator)

Level	Conditioning	Parameters
Field	No	1) Time separator

This keyword overrides the time separator for the display file time field.

PARAMETER DEFINITION

Time separator
This parameter is either an explicit value defined within apostrophes (') or a value of *JOB. The valid values are colon (:), period (.), and blank ( ). *JOB indicates you are to use the job's default separator.

```
....1....+....2....+....3....+....4....+....5....+....6....+....7....+....8
A            R FORMAT1
A              TIMFLD1       T    10 10TIMFMT(*ISO)
A              TIMFLD2       T    12 10TIMFMT(*USA)
A              TIMFLD3       T    14 10TIMFMT(*HMS)
A                                    TIMSEP(':')
```

UNLOCK (Unlock)

Level	Conditioning	Parameters
Record	No	1) Input clearing (optional)

This keyword keeps the keyboard unlocked when you perform a read against the record format. Normally, the keyboard is locked when control is returned to your HLL program.

This keyword also works with the GETRETAIN keyword to determine how input fields on the screen should be treated.

PARAMETER DEFINITION

Input clearing

This parameter is optional and can have one or both of the following values: *ERASE and *MDTOFF. *ERASE indicates that all input-capable fields are to be cleared. *MDTOFF leaves the data alone but turns off all modified data tags for all input-capable fields. *ERASE is the default.

The table below shows the effect this keyword has when used with and without the GETRETAIN keyword.

UNLOCK Parameter	Without GETRETAIN	With GETRETAIN
None	Input fields are erased. MDTs remain on.	Input fields not erased. MDTs are turned off.
(*ERASE)	Input fields are erased. MDTs remain on.	Invalid
(*MDTOFF)	Input fields are not erased MDTs are turned off.	Invalid
(*ERASE *MDTOFF)	All input fields with MDTs on are erased. MDTs are turned off.	Invalid
(*MDTOFF *ERASE)	All input fields with MDTs on are erased. MDTs are turned off.	Invalid

USER (User)

Level	Conditioning	Parameters
Field	No	None

This keyword displays the current user profile name on the screen in a ten-character field.

```
....1....+....2....+....3....+....4....+....5....+....6....+....7....+....8
A          R FORMAT1
A                                    1 62'User:'
A                                    1 72USER
```

USRDFN (User Defined)

Level	Conditioning	Parameters
Record	No	None

This keyword specifies that the record format contains user-defined data streams. No fields are allowed in the record format when you use this keyword.

```
....1....+....2....+....3....+....4....+....5....+....6....+....7....+....8
A          R FORMAT1
A                                        USRDFN
```

USRDSPMGT (User Display Management)

Level	Conditioning	Parameters
File	No	None

You can use this keyword in the System/36 Environment to indicate that all data written to the display is not to be cleared until it is explicitly overwritten or cleared with the CLRL keyword.

```
....1....+....2....+....3....+....4....+....5....+....6....+....7....+....8
A                                        USRDSPMGT
A          R FORMAT1
```

USRRSTDSP (User Restore Display)

Level	Conditioning	Parameters
Record	Yes	None

This keyword specifies that background screens are not automatically saved and restored when windows are being used. Your application is responsible for re-establishing the background image on the screen.

When you use this keyword, you are no longer limited to 12 active windows at one time, although only 12 can be displayed at the same time.

```
....1....+....2....+....3....+....4....+....5....+....6....+....7....+....8
A           R FORMAT1
A   40                              USRRSTDSP
A                                   WINDOW(10 10 5 50)
```

VALNUM (Validate Numeric)

Level	Conditioning	Parameters
File	No	None
Record		
Field		

This keyword prevents the user from entering a space, plus sign (+), or minus sign (-) between digits. It also prevents the user from entering a plus sign (+) or minus sign (-) before the number. VALNUM is valid only on fields of data type Y.

```
....1....+....2....+....3....+....4....+....5....+....6....+....7....+....8
A           R FORMAT1
A             FIELD1       4Y 0B 10 10VALNUM
```

VALUES (Values)

Level	Conditioning	Parameters
Field	No	1) Value list

This keyword specifies a list of valid values for a field.

PARAMETER DEFINITION

Value list
This parameter is a list of up to 100 entries against which you can validate the field.

```
....1....+....2....+....3....+....4....+....5....+....6....+....7....+....8
A           R FORMAT1
A             STATUS       1A  B 10 10VALUES('M' 'S' 'W' 'D')
A             CODE         2Y 0B 10 20VALUES(10 15 18 24 32)
```

VLDCMDKEY (Valid Command Key)

Level	Conditioning	Parameters
Record	No	1) Response indicator
		2) Text (optional)

This keyword notifies your HLL program when the user has pressed a valid command key. The valid command keys are ALTHELP, ALTPAGEUP, ALTPAGEDWN, CA*nn*, CF*nn*, CLEAR, HELP, HOME, PAGEDOWN, PAGEUP, PRINT, ROLLUP, and ROLLDOWN.

PARAMETER DEFINITIONS

Response indicator
This parameter is the indicator to be turned on when the user presses a valid command key. The valid values are 01 to 99.

Text
The text parameter contains up to 50 characters of text to serve as documentation for the keyword. You code the text within apostrophes (').

```
....1....+....2....+....3....+....4....+....5....+....6....+....7....+....8
A          R FORMAT1                  VLDCMDKEY(44 'Enter not pressed')
A                                     CF03(03 'Exit Requested')
```

WDWBORDER (Window Border)

Level	Conditioning	Parameters
File	Yes	1) Color (optional)
		2) Display attribute (optional)
		3) Characters (optional)

This keyword defines the attributes of a window's border.

PARAMETER DEFINITIONS

Color
This parameter specifies the color to be used for the window border. This parameter has two elements: *COLOR and one of the following color identifiers:

(*COLOR GRN)	Green
(*COLOR RED)	Red
(*COLOR BLU)	Blue
(*COLOR WHT)	White
(*COLOR TRQ)	Turquoise
(*COLOR YLW)	Yellow
(*COLOR PNK)	Pink

The default color is blue.

Display attribute

This parameter specifies the display attribute to be used for the window border. This parameter has two elements: *DSPATR and one of the following display attributes:

(*DSPATR BL)	Blink
(*DSPATR CS)	Column Separator
(*DSPATR HI)	High Intensity
(*DSPATR ND)	Nondisplay
(*DSPATR RI)	Reverse Image
(*DSPATR UL)	Underline

The default display attribute is normal video.

You can specify more than one display attribute after the *DSPATR code (e.g., *DSPATR HI RI).

Characters

This optional parameter defines the characters used to build the border. You express this parameter in the format (*CHAR 'characters'). The characters within the apostrophes are eight units long. Each character position represents one part of the border. The following table shows which positions represent which parts of the border:

Character Position	Border Position
1	Top-left corner
2	Top border
3	Top-right corner
4	Left border
5	Right border
6	Bottom-left corner
7	Bottom border
8	Bottom-right corner

The default is a period (.) for each side and a colon (:) for each corner.

```
....1....+....2....+....3....+....4....+....5....+....6....+....7....+....8
A          R FORMAT1              WINDOW(10 10 5 50)
A    40                           WDWBORDER((*DSPATR RI) +
A                                 (*CHAR '        '))
```

WDWTITLE (Window Title)

Level	Conditioning	Parameters
Record	Yes	1) Title text (optional)
		2) Color (optional)
		3) Display attribute (optional)
		4) Positioning (optional)
		5) Location (optional)
		NOTE: At least one parameter must be specified.

This keyword defines a title for a window.

PARAMETER DEFINITIONS

Title text

This optional parameter specifies the text to be displayed. This parameter has two elements: *TEXT and the actual text to be displayed. The text is entered within apostrophes ('). You can also use a variable field to specify the text. In this case, the field must be defined in the same record format and have a data type of A and a usage of P.

If the text exceeds the window size, the text is truncated.

Color

This optional parameter specifies the color to be used for the title text. This parameter has two elements: *COLOR and one of the following color identifiers:

(*COLOR GRN)	Green
(*COLOR RED)	Red
(*COLOR BLU)	Blue
(*COLOR WHT)	White
(*COLOR TRQ)	Turquoise
(*COLOR YLW)	Yellow
(*COLOR PNK)	Pink

The default color is the color of the border.

Display attribute

This optional parameter specifies the display attribute to be used for the title text. This parameter has two elements: *DSPATR and one of the following display attributes:

(*DSPATR BL)	Blink
(*DSPATR CS)	Column Separator
(*DSPATR HI)	High Intensity
(*DSPATR ND)	Nondisplay
(*DSPATR RI)	Reverse Image
(*DSPATR UL)	Underline

The default display attribute is the display attribute of the border.

You can specify more than one display attribute after the *DSPATR code (e.g., *DSPATR HI RI).

Positioning

This optional parameter specifies how the text is positioned on the line. The valid values are *CENTER, *LEFT, and *RIGHT.

When the location is *TOP, the default positioning is *CENTER; it is *LEFT when the location is *BOTTOM.

Location

This optional parameter specifies on which line the text will appear. The valid values are *TOP (the default) and *BOTTOM.

```
....1....+....2....+....3....+....4....+....5....+....6....+....7....+....8
A           R FORMAT1                     WINDOW(10 10 5 50)
A    40                                   WDWTITLE((*TEXT 'Title' ) +
A                                         (*COLOR RED))
A    41                                   WDWTITLE((*TEXT &TITLE) +
A                                         (*COLOR WHT) (*DSPATR UL) +
A                                         *RIGHT *BOTTOM)
```

WINDOW (Window)

Level	Conditioning	Parameters
Record	No	NOTE: This keyword has two formats.
		Explicit Window:
		1) Starting line
		2) Starting column
		3) Window lines
		4) Window columns
		5) Message line (optional)
		6) Restrict cursor (optional)
		Referenced Window:
		1) Record format

This keyword defines a window on the screen. You can use one of two formats. The first explicitly defines the window area; the second references another record format that in turn defines a window.

PARAMETER DEFINITIONS: EXPLICIT WINDOW

Starting line

This parameter specifies on which display line the upper left corner of the window is to be placed. In addition to hard-coding a starting line, you can use a variable field to specify the starting line at runtime. If you use a variable field, it must be defined in the same record format, have a data type of S, be no more than three digits long with zero decimal positions, and have a usage of P.

You can specify a special value of *DFT in place of the starting-line reference. *DFT uses the cursor's current location on the screen to determine the upper left corner of the window. If you use *DFT, you do not specify the starting column parameter.

Starting column

This parameter specifies on which display column the upper left corner of the window is to be placed. You do not specify this parameter if you use *DFT for the starting-line parameter. You can also use a variable field to specify the starting column. the variable field must be defined in the same record format, have a data type of S, be no more than three digits long with zero decimal positions, and have a usage of P.

Window lines

This parameter specifies the number of lines the window occupies on the screen. This number does not include the window borders.

Window columns

This parameter defines the number of columns the window occupies on the screen. This number does not include the window borders nor the beginning and ending attribute positions needed for each line.

Message line

This optional parameter specifies where the message line is to be placed on the screen. The valid values are *MSGLIN and *NOMSGLIN. *MSGLIN indicates that the message line is on the last line of the active window. *NOMSGLIN uses the default message line defined for the display file; the default is *MSGLIN.

Restrict cursor

This optional parameter indicates whether to let the user have full or partial access to functions defined by the window. The values are *RSTCSR and *NORSTCSR.

*RSTCSR restricts the user from performing functions when the cursor is outside the window area. *NORSTCSR lets the user have full access to window-defined functions regardless of the cursor location. *RSTCSR is the default.

PARAMETER DEFINITION: REFERENCED WINDOW

Record format
This parameter specifies the name of a record format that contains the window definition to be used by this record format.

```
....1....+....2....+....3....+....4...+....5....+....6....+....7....+....8
A          R FORMAT1                    WINDOW(10 10 5 50 *NOMSGLIN +
A                                       *NORSTCSR)

A          R FORMAT2                    WINDOW(&ROW &COL 5 50)
A            ROW           3S  0P
A            COL           3S  0P

A          R FORMAT3                    WINDOW(10 10 5 50)

A          R FORMAT4                    WINDOW(FORMAT3)
```

WRDWRAP (Word Wrap)

Level	Conditioning	Parameters
File	No	None
Record		
Field		

This keyword specifies that fields that occupy more than one line of the display are to be wrapped, if necessary, at blanks instead of in the middle of a word. This keyword is similar in function to the BLKFOLD keyword but is valid only for input-capable fields.

```
....1....+....2....+....3....+....4....+....5....+....6....+....7....+....8
A          R FORMAT1
A            FIELD1       600A  B  1 10WRDWRAP
```

Chapter 4

Printer Files

Printer files are used to define output specifications that are external to your HLL program. Basic printing functions are very easy to understand and use.

DATA STREAMS

When considering printer files, you must keep in mind that there are basically three different types of print (referred to as data streams): Single Character Set (SCS), Intelligent Printer Data Stream (IPDS) and Advanced Function Printing (AFP).

SCS refers to standard line, dot-matrix, or laser printers. IPDS and AFP data streams will not print on these printers.

IPDS refers to physical printers capable of printing IBM IPDS data. The device description of the printer must be created with DEVTYPE(*IPDS) on the CRTDEVPRT command. IPDS is a subset of AFP. IPDS data streams can handle SCS data but not AFP-specific data streams.

AFP refers to physical printers capable of printing IPDS data; these printers will also use the AS/400 CPU to format the print. The device description of the printer must be created with DEVTYPE(*IPDS) and AFP(*YES) on the CRTDEVPRT command. With V3R1, AFP is an orderable feature.

DATA TYPES

The following table shows the valid data types (column 35) for printer files:

Code	Meaning
S	Zoned decimal
F	Floating point
A	Character
L	Date Field
T	Time Field
Z	Timestamp Field

If you don't specify a data type, the default will be A for character fields and S for numeric fields.

FIELD USAGE

The following table shows what field usages (column 38) are available for printer files:

Code	Meaning
blank	Output
O	Output
P	Program-to-system field

KEYWORD LEVELS

Printer files have three distinct levels in which keywords can be specified. These are file level, record-format level, and field level.

File level refers to those keywords that will affect the entire printer file. The keywords are placed ahead of the first record format in the DDS source.

Record-format level refers to those keywords that affect the format of the printer file. A record format is defined by placing an R in column 17 of the A-spec. These keywords are placed ahead of the first field definition in the record format.

Field level refers to those keywords that affect an individual field within the record format.

KEYWORDS

The column "Conditioning" in the following tables indicates whether you are allowed to specify indicators in columns 7-16.

The column "Data Stream" in the tables indicates the minimum data stream requirements for using the keyword.

ALIAS (Alternative Name)

Level	Conditioning	DataStream	Parameters
Field	No	SCS	1) Alternate-name

This keyword lets you assign a name longer than 10 characters for a field. If your HLL program (e.g., Cobol, PL/1) provides support for longer field names, this alias definition will be used; otherwise, it is ignored.

PARAMETER DEFINITION

Alternate-name

For this parameter, the alternate name specified can be up to 30 characters in length.

```
....1....+....2....+....3....+....4....+....5....+....6....+....7....+....8
A          R FORMAT1
A            CUSNBR        7S 0   10 10ALIAS(CUSTOMER_NUMBER)
A            CUSNAM       35A     10 20ALIAS(CUSTOMER_NAME)
```

BARCODE (Bar Code)

Level	Conditioning	Data Stream	Parameters
Field	No	IPDS	1) Bar-code-id
			2) Height (Optional)
			3) Direction (Optional)
			4) Human-readable (Optional)
			5) Asterisk (Optional)
			6) Check-digit (Optional)
			7) Unit-width (Optional)
			8) Ratio (Optional)

This keyword generates a bar code on the printed page. Some bar codes are valid only for numeric fields (data type S); others are valid for character fields only (data type A).

PARAMETER DEFINITIONS

Bar-code-id

This parameter is a code indicating the type of bar code to generate. The following table lists valid codes and the corresponding data type:

Code	Data Type and Size
MSI	Numeric — up to 31 digits
UPCA	Numeric — 11 digits
UPCE	Numeric — 10 digits
UPC2	Numeric — 2 digits (Must follow UPCA or UPCE)
UPC5	Numeric — 5 digits (Must follow UPCA or UPCE)
EAN8	Numeric — 7 digits
EAN13	Numeric — 12 digits
EAN2	Numeric — 2 digits (Must follow EAN8 or EAN13
EAN5	Numeric — 5 digits (Must follow EAN8 or EAN13
CODEABAR	Alphanumeric — up to 50 characters
CODE128	Alphanumeric — up to 50 characters
CODE3OF9	Alphanumeric — up to 50 characters
INTERL2OF5	Numeric — up to 31 digits
INDUST2OF5	Numeric — up to 31 digits
MATRIX2OF5	Numeric — up to 31 digits
POSTNET	Numeric — up to 31 digits
RM4SCC	Alphanumeric — up to 31 characters
JPBC	Alphanumeric — up to 50 characters

Height

This optional parameter specifies the height of the bar code when it is printed. This number is between 1 and 9, which represents the number of lines the bar code will occupy. This parameter, if specified, must come after the bar-code-id.
The following parameters can be specified in any order.

Direction

This parameter indicates the direction on the page in which the bar code will be printed. The valid values are *HRZ for horizontal and *VRT for vertical. The default is *HRZ.

Human-readable

This parameter indicates whether the human-readable text of the bar code should be printed and, if so, where. The valid values are *HRI for print human-readable below the bar code, *HRITOP for print human-readable above the bar code, and *NOHRI for don't print human-readable text. The default is *HRI.

Asterisk

This parameter indicates whether to include the asterisk for CODE3OF9 bar codes. The valid values are *AST for include asterisk and *NOAST for exclude asterisk. The default is *NOAST.

Check-digit

This parameter indicates whether you want to include a check digit with the bar code. Check-digit is a one-byte value. The value of X'FF' is not allowed.

Unit-width

This parameter indicates the width in inches of the narrow bar/space. It would be expressed as (*WIDTH .nnn), where *nnn* is between .007 and .208.

Ratio

This parameter indicates the ratio of wide bar/space to the narrow bar/space. It would be expressed as (*RATIO n.nn), where *n.nn* is a value between 2.00 and 3.00.

```
....1....+....2....+....3....+....4....+....5....+....6....+....7....+....8
A          R FORMAT1
A            PART#        10A    10 10BARCODE(CODE3OF9 3)
A            UPC          11S 0  20 10BARCODE(UPCA 3 (*RATIO 2.5) +
A                                   *HRZ (*WIDTH .105) *HRITOP)
```

BLKFOLD (Blank Fold)

Level	Conditioning	DataStream	Parameters
Field	No	SCS (only)	None

This keyword causes a long field to print on multiple lines at a blank within a field rather than just at the end of the line. This keyword will not work unless FOLD(*YES) has been specified on the CRTPRTF, CHGPRTF, or OVRPRTF commands.

This keyword is not valid for IPDS or AFP data streams.

```
....1....+....2....+....3....+....4....+....5....+....6....+....7....+....8
A          R FORMAT1
A            NOTE          300A    10 10BLKFOLD
```

BOX (Box)

Level	Conditioning	DataStream	Parameters
Record	Yes	AFP	1) Corner-down
			2) Corner-across
			3) Diagonal-down
			4) Diagonal-across
			5) Line-width

This keyword prints a rectangular box on a page. BOX is valid only for AFP data streams. You define the box by specifying two corners of the box. These corners must be diagonal from each other.

PARAMETER DEFINITIONS

Corner-down
This parameter is the vertical starting point of the box, down from the top of the margins set. The valid values are 0-57.790 cm or 0-22.750 inches.

Corner-across
This parameter is the horizontal starting point of the box, across the page from the left margin. The valid values are 0-57.790 cm or 0-22.750 inches.

Diagonal-down
This parameter is the location (down from the top of the margins set) of the horizontal corner that is diagonal from the first corner points defined. The valid values are 0-57.790 cm or 0-22.750 inches.

Diagonal-across

This parameter is the location (across from the left margin set) of the vertical corner that is diagonal from the first corner points defined. The valid values are 0-57.790 cm or 0-22.750 inches.

Line-width

This parameter defines how wide the line is to be when the box is printed. Its value can be from 0-57.790 cm or 0-22.750 inches. You can also use the following special values:

Value	Line Width
*NARROW	12/1440 in. (.008 in, .022 cm)
*MEDIUM	24/1440 in. (.017 in, .042 cm)
*WIDE	36/1440 in. (.025 in, .064 cm)

```
....1....+....2....+....3....+....4....+....5....+....6....+....7....+....8
A            R FORMAT1                      BOX(1 1 3 3 *MEDIUM)
A   40                                      BOX(0 0 8.5 11.0 .5)
```

CDEFNT (Coded Font Name)

Level	Conditioning	DataStream	Parameters
Record	Yes	AFP	1) Coded-font-name
Field			2) Point size (optional)

This keyword specifies a coded font for the printing of a field or a specific record format. Coded fonts are character definitions that are different from those normally used. This keyword is valid only for AFP data streams.

PARAMETER DEFINITIONS

Coded-font-name

This parameter is the name of the external coded font to be used. You can optionally specify the library name where the coded font is found.

Point-size

This optional parameter further defines a numeric font. This parameter is expressed as (*POINTSIZE n.n) where *n.n* is a number between 0.1 and 999.9.

```
....1....+....2....+....3....+....4....+....5....+....6....+....7....+....8
A            R FORMAT1                      CDEFNT(FONT2)
A              CUSNAM        35A      10 20CDEFNT(FONTLIB/FONT10)
```

CHRID (Character Identifier)

Level	Conditioning	DataStream	Parameters
Field	No	SCS	None
		IPDS	
		AFP	

This keyword indicates that a different character set can be used from the default for the print device. The character set to use is defined by the CHRID parameter on the CRTPRTF, CHGPRTF, or OVRPRTF commands. This keyword has different rules depending on the data stream.

When CHRID is used with SCS data streams, you cannot specify this keyword in connection with the DFNCHR or TRNSPY keywords.

When CHRID is used with IPDS data streams, you can use it with the TRNSPY keyword.

When CHRID is used with AFP, you can only use registered font IDs. This means that if other fonts have been downloaded installed in your AS/400, you cannot use them with this keyword.

```
....1....+....2....+....3....+....4....+....5....+....6....+....7....+....8
A          R FORMAT1
A            CUSNAM        35A    10 20CHRID
```

CHRSIZ (Character Size)

Level	Conditioning	DataStream	Parameters
Record	No	IPDS	1) Width
Field			2) Height

This keyword lets you print characters larger than normal.

PARAMETER DEFINITIONS

Width
This parameter is a number between 1.0 and 20.0 that indicates how wide to make each character. To get the new width, multiply the current character width (as determined by the font and lines-per-inch settings) by this number.

Height
This parameter is a number between 1.0 and 20.0 that indicates how high to make each character. To get the new height, multiply the current character height (as determined by the font and lines-per-inch settings) by this number.

```
....1....+....2....+....3....+....4....+....5....+....6....+....7....+....8
A          R FORMAT1
A            TITLE         10A    10 10CHRSIZ(3 3)
```

COLOR (Color)

Level	Conditioning	DataStream	Parameters
Field	Yes	IPDS	1) Color

This keyword lets you print in color if the printer supports that feature. This keyword will be ignored for SCS data streams.

PARAMETER DEFINITION

Color

This value indicates the color you wish to print.

The following table shows valid values for this parameter and their meaning:

Color	Meaning
BLK	Black
BLU	Blue
BRN	Brown
GRN	Green
PNK	Pink
RED	Red
TRQ	Turquoise

```
....1....+....2....+....3....+....4....+....5....+....6....+....7....+....8
A           R FORMAT1
A             CUSNBR       7S 0  10 10COLOR(GRN)
A             CUSNAM       35A    10 20
A    40                            COLOR(RED)
```

CPI (Characters Per Inch)

Level	Conditioning	DataStream	Parameters
Record	Yes	SCS(only)	1) Characters-per-inch
Field			

This keyword changes the default characters per inch (as determined by the CPI parameter on the CRTPRTF, CHGPRTF, and OVRPRTF commands). This keyword will work only for 5224 and 5225 SCS printers.

PARAMETER DEFINITION

Characters-per-inch

This parameter is a value of 10 or 15.

```
....1....+....2....+....3....+....4....+....5....+....6....+....7....+....8
A           R FORMAT1                 CPI(10)
A             CUSNBR       7S 0  10 10
A             CUSNAM       35A    10 20CPI(15)
```

CVTDTA (Convert Data)

Level	Conditioning	DataStream	Parameters
Field	No	SCS	None
		IPDS	

This keyword converts data to hexadecimal data when the field is passed to
the printer. This keyword has different functions when used with SCS and
IPDS printers.

For SCS printers, you only use this keyword with the DFNCHR keyword;
you must specify the TRNSPY keyword as well.

For IPDS printers, you can use this keyword on any character field.

The field size defined in your DDS must be twice the size of the actual
data being sent. For example, if you are sending four characters, the field must
be eight characters in length in your DDS.

```
....1....+....2....+....3....+....4....+....5....+....6....+....7....+....8
A            R FORMAT1                    DFNCHR(x'51' 'FF00FF00FF00FF00FF')
A              FIELD        2A      10 10CVTDTA    TRNSPY
```

```
....1....+....2....+....3....+....4....+....5....+....6....+....7....+....8
A            R FORMAT1
A              FIELD       10A      10 10CVTDTA
```

DATE (Date)

Level	Conditioning	DataStream	Parameters
Field	No	SCS	1) Date-choice (Optional)

This keyword prints a date.

PARAMETER DEFINITION

Date-choice
This optional parameter indicates whether you wish to print the job date or the
system date. The valid values are *JOB for job date and *SYS for the system date.
The default is *JOB.

```
....1....+....2....+....3....+....4....+....5....+....6....+....7....+....8
A            R FORMAT1
A                               1120DATE
```

DATFMT (Date Format)

Level	Conditioning	DataStream	Parameters
Field	No	SCS	1) Date-format

This keyword lets you specify the format of a date field. This keyword can only be specified on a field with a data type of L.

PARAMETER DEFINITION

Date-format

This parameter defines how the date will appear on the report. The following are the valid values for this parameter:

Date-Format	Meaning	Format
*JOB	Job default	
*YMD	Year/Month/Day	yy/mm/dd
*MDY	Month/Day/Year	mm/dd/yy
*DMY	Day/Month/Year	dd/mm/yy
*JUL	Julian	yy/ddd
*ISO	International Standards Organization	yyyy-mm-dd
*USA	USA standard	mm/dd/yyyy
*EUR	European standard	dd.mm.yyyy
*JIS	Japanese Industrial standard	yyyy-mm-dd

```
....1....+....2....+....3....+....4....+....5....+....6....+....7....+....8
A          R FORMAT1
A            FIELD1          L    10 10DATFMT(*ISO)
```

DATSEP (Date Separator)

Level	Conditioning	DataStream	Parameters
Field	No	SCS	1) Date-separator

This keyword defines the separator to be used for a date field (data type L). If the date field is defined as *ISO, *USA, *EUR, or *JIS, you cannot specify this keyword.

PARAMETER DEFINITION

Date-separator

This parameter is either an explicit value defined within single quotes (') or a value of *JOB. The valid values are slash (/), dash (-), period (.), comma (,), or blank ( ). *JOB indicates you are to use the default found for the job.

```
....1....+....2....+....3....+....4....+....5....+....6....+....7....+....8
A          R FORMAT1
A            FIELD1          L    10 10DATFMT(*YMD)
A                                   DATSEP('.')
```

DFNCHR (Define Character)

Level	Conditioning	DataStream	Parameters
File	Yes	SCS(only)	1) Code-point
Record			2) Matrix-pattern

This keyword lets you redefine a print character for 5224 and 5225 dot-matrix printers. Whenever the redefined character is printed, the new definition is used.

You must specify the TRNSPY keyword on any literal or field that can generate the redefined character.

If a field can send the redefined character, you must also specify the CVTDTA keyword for that field.

PARAMETER DEFINITIONS

Code-point
This parameter is a hexadecimal value of the character that is to be redefined. This value is entered in the format of x'nn', where *nn* is a valid hex value.

Matrix-pattern
This parameter is a string of nine characters that maps to the redefined image to be printed. You enter the characters in their hexadecimal format, thus requiring that 18 characters be entered in this parameter.

You can specify up to 50 code-point/matrix-pattern definitions within a single DFNCHR keyword.

```
....1....+....2....+....3....+....4....+....5....+....6....+....7....+....8
A          R FORMAT1                     DFNCHR(x'51' 'FF00FF00FF00FF00FF')
A            FIELD           2A    10 10CVTDTA    TRNSPY
A                                  20 20DFT(X'51')   TRNSPY
```

DFT (Default)

Level	Conditioning	DataStream	Parameters
Field	No	SCS	1) Value

This keyword lets you specify a default print value for the output. However, you can explicitly define a literal without this keyword.

PARAMETER DEFINITION

Value
This parameter is the value you wish to print, and it must be enclosed within single quotes ('). You can also specify a hexadecimal value string.

```
....1....+....2....+....3....+....4....+....5....+....6....+....7....+....8
A          R FORMAT1
A                                    10 10DFT('Hi')
A                                    10 20DFT(x'7C')
```

DLTEDT (Delete Edit)

Level	Conditioning	DataStream	Parameters
Field	No	SCS	None

You use this keyword to remove EDTCDE and EDTWRD definitions that would normally be copied when you are formatting a referenced field.

```
....1....+....2....+....3....+....4....+....5....+....6....+....7....+....8
A          R FORMAT1
A            CUSNBR      R          REFFLD(CUST# REFFILE)
A                                   DLTEDT
```

DRAWER (Drawer)

Level	Conditioning	DataStream	Parameters
Record	Yes	SCS	1) Drawer-number

This keyword lets you specify which paper drawer is to be used for single-sheet-fed printers. This keyword will override the DRAWER parameter on the CRTPRTF, CHGPRTF, and OVRPRTF commands.

PARAMETER DEFINITION

Drawer-number

This parameter is a number between 1 and 255 that indicates from which drawer paper will be drawn. You can also specify a value of *E1, which indicates that the envelope drawer is to be used.

```
....1....+....2....+....3....+....4....+....5....+....6....+....7....+....8
A          R FORMAT1
A  40                                DRAWER(1)
A  41                                DRAWER(2)
A            CUSNBR     7S 0  10 10
A            CUSNAM     35A   10 20
```

DTASTMCMD (Data Stream Command)

Level	Conditioning	DataStream	Parameters
Record	Yes	AFPDS	1) Text
Field			

This keyword is used to store a data stream command or other piece of data into a spool file. The spool file could then be processed by a user application program that can process the spool file based on the embedded data. This data will have no direct effect on the actual spool file when it is printed.

PARAMETER DEFINITION

Text

This parameter defines the text to be embedded. This can either be a hard-coded value or can be defined using a program-to-system variable.

EDTCDE (Edit Code)

Level	Conditioning	DataStream	Parameters
Field	No	SCS	1) Edit-code
			2) Floating-character (Optional)

This keyword defines the format a numeric field will have when printed. Each edit code has a different effect on how the data will be printed.

PARAMETER DEFINITION

Edit-code

This parameter is a valid AS/400 edit code. The following are the valid codes and their effect on the number when it is printed:

Code	Commas Printed	Decimal Points Printed	Negative Sign Shown	Zero Value
1	Yes	Yes	No Sign	0 printed
2	Yes	Yes	No Sign	Blanks
3	No	Yes	No Sign	0 printed
4	No	Yes	No Sign	Blanks
A	Yes	Yes	CR	0 printed
B	Yes	Yes	CR	Blanks
C	No	Yes	CR	0 printed
D	No	Yes	CR	Blanks
J	Yes	Yes	- (Minus)	0 printed
K	Yes	Yes	- (Minus)	Blanks
L	No	Yes	- (Minus)	0 printed
M	No	Yes	- (Minus)	Blanks
N	Yes	Yes	- (Minus)	0 printed
O	Yes	Yes	- (Minus)	Blanks
P	No	Yes	- (Minus)	0 printed

continued

Code	Commas Printed	Decimal Points Printed	Negative Sign Shown	Zero Value
Q	No	Yes	- (Minus)	Blanks
W	No	No	Blank	0/000
Y	No	No	Blank	0/00/00
Z	No	No	Blank	Blanks

Edit codes J-M will place the minus sign after the number. Edit codes N-Q will place the minus sign before the number.

The W edit code is used to suppress the leftmost digit of a date field that is five digits long, the three leftmost digits of a date field six to eight digits long. The W edit code will place a slash (/) between the year, month, and day data in the date field.

The Y edit code is similar to the W edit code but is used with fields that contain date value not date fields.

The Y edit code is used with fields that contain dates.

Floating-character
This optional parameter is either an asterisk (*) or any other character designated to act as a floating currency symbol. An asterisk indicates that the numeric field is to have all leading zeros replaced with asterisks. The floating character will appear to the left of the most significant digit.

```
....1....+....2....+....3....+....4....+....5....+....6....+....7....+....8
A            R FORMAT1
A              CUSNBR       7P 0  10 10EDTCDE(4)
A              CUSNAM      35A    10 25
A              ORDNBR       7P 0  11 10EDTCDE(4)
A              SLSAMT       9P 2  11 45EDTCDE(L)
```

EDTWRD (Edit Word)

Level	Conditioning	DataStream	Parameters
Field	No	SCS	1) Edit-word

This keyword creates a special edit description for a numeric field when one of the AS/400 edit codes does not provide the formatting you need.

PARAMETER DEFINITION

Edit-word
This is a valid AS/400 edit-word character string.

```
....1....+....2....+....3....+....4....+....5....+....6....+....7....+....8
A              R FORMAT1
A                EMP#          7P 0  10 10
A                EMPNAM       35A     10 25
A                SSN           9P 0  11 10EDTWRD('   -  -    ')
```

ENDPAGE (End Page)

Level	Conditioning	DataStream	Parameters
Record	Yes	AFP	None

This keyword ejects the current page after the record format is printed. This keyword is valid only with AFP data streams. You cannot use this keyword with the SKIPA, SKIPB, SPACEA, or SPACEB keywords.

```
....1....+....2....+....3....+....4....+....5....+....6....+....7....+....8
A              R FORMAT1
A   40                                        ENDPAGE
A                CUSNBR        7S 0  10 10
A                CUSNAM       35A     10 20
```

FLTFIXDEC (Floating-Point to Fixed-Decimal)

Level	Conditioning	DataStream	Parameters
Field	No	SCS	None

This keyword prints a floating-point number in fixed-decimal notation. The number will print in fixed-decimal notation only if the value is small enough; otherwise, it will print in standard floating-point form.

```
....1....+....2....+....3....+....4....+....5....+....6....+....7....+....8
A              R FORMAT1
A                FIELD1        8F 3  10 10FLTFIXDEC
```

FLTPCN (Floating-Point Precision)

Level	Conditioning	DataStream	Parameters
Field	No	SCS	1) Precision

This keyword specifies the precision or size of a floating-point number when the number is printed.

PARAMETER DEFINITION

Precision

This parameter is a value of *SINGLE or *DOUBLE. *SINGLE floating-point numbers can be up to 9 digits in length. *DOUBLE floating-point numbers can be up to 17 digits long.

```
....1....+....2....+....3....+....4....+....5....+....6....+....7....+....8
A          R FORMAT1
A            FIELD1        17F 5   1Ø 1ØFLTPCN(*DOUBLE)
```

FNTCHRSET (Font Character Set)

Level	Conditioning	DataStream	Parameters
Record	Yes	AFP	1) Font-character-set
Field			2) Code-page
			3) Point-size

This keyword specifies the font to be used for printing a field or literal. This keyword will only work with AFP data streams.

PARAMETER DEFINITIONS

Font-character-set

This parameter is the name of the font character set. You can optionally specify the library where the font character set is found.

Code-page

This is the name of the code page to be used with the font. You can optionally specify the library where the code page is found.

The font character set and code page are validated at print time, not at compile time.

Point-size

This optional parameter further defines a numeric font. This parameter is expressed as (*POINTSIZE n.n) where *n.n* is a number between 0.1 and 999.9.

```
....1....+....2....+....3....+....4....+....5....+....6....+....7....+....8
A          R FORMAT1
A                                      FONT(FONTLIB/FONTSET3 CODELIB/CODEP+
A                                      3)
A            CUSNBR        7S Ø   1Ø 1Ø
A            CUSNAM       35A   1Ø 2ØFONT(FONTSET1 CODEP1)
```

FONT (Font)

Level	Conditioning	DataStream	Parameters
Record	Yes	SCS	1) Font-identifier
Field			2) Point-size (Optional)

This keyword specifies a font ID that will be used to print a field or literal. This keyword is used to override the FONT parameter on the CRTPRTF, CHGPRTF, and OVRPRTF commands.

PARAMETER DEFINITIONS

Font-identifier

This parameter is the ID of the font to use. This will be either a numeric font identifier assigned by the AS/400, a graphic font name, or a value of *VECTOR.

*VECTOR is used in connection with 4234 IPDS printers only.

Point-size

This optional parameter further defines a numeric font. This parameter is expressed as (*POINTSIZE n.n) where *n.n* is a number between 0.1 and 999.9.

```
....1....+....2....+....3....+....4....+....5....+....6....+....7....+....8
A           R FORMAT1
A             CUSNBR        7S 0   10 10
A             CUSNAM        35A    10 20FONT(222)
```

GDF (Graphic Data File)

Level	Conditioning	DataStream	Parameters
Record	Yes	AFP	1) Graphic-file
			2) Graphic-member
			3) Position-down
			4) Position-across
			5) Graph-depth
			6) Graph-width
			7) Graph-rotation

This keyword prints a graphic data file. GDF is valid only for AFP data streams.

PARAMETER DEFINITIONS

Graphic-file

This parameter is the name of the graphic file to print. You can optionally specify the library where the graphic data file is found. You can also use a variable field to specify the name of the graphic data file and/or library. If you use a variable field, the field must be defined within the same record format, have a data type of A, be 10 characters in length, and have a usage of P.

Graphic-member

This parameter is the name of the member to use within the graphic data file. You can use a variable field to specify the member name. If you use a variable field, you must use the same definition rules as for the graphic-file parameter.

Position-down

This parameter specifies the vertical starting position of the graphic data file to be printed. This is the position down from the top of the page margin. The valid values are 0-22.75 for inches and 0-57.79 for centimeters.

You can also specify this parameter via a variable name. If you do so, that field name must be defined within the same record format, have a data type of S, be five digits in length with three decimal positions, and have a usage of P.

Position-across

This parameter specifies the horizontal starting position of the graphic data file to be printed. This is the position across from the left margin of the page. The valid values are 0-22.75 for inches and 0-57.79 for centimeters.

You can also specify this parameter via a variable. To do so, you would use the same rules as for the position-down parameter.

Graph-depth

This parameter defines the depth of the chart, thus causing the chart to be scaled to fit within the area defined. The valid values are 0-22.75 for inches and 0-57.79 for centimeters.

You can also specify this parameter via a variable. To do so, you would use the same rules as for the position-down and position-across parameters.

Graph-width

This parameter defines the width of the chart, thus causing the chart to be scaled to fit within the area defined. The valid values are 0-22.75 for inches and 0-57.79 for centimeters.

You can also specify this parameter via a variable. To do so, you would use the same rules as for the position-down, position-across, and graph-depth parameters.

Graph-rotation

This parameter specifies the rotation of the chart on the printed page. The valid values are 0, 90, 180, and 270.

```
....1....+....2....+....3....+....4....+....5....+....6....+....7....+....8
A           R FORMAT1
A                                          GDF(CHART1 MEMBER1 0 0 5 5 0)
A                                          GDF(&LIB/&FILE &MBR &DOWN &ACROSS +
A                                          &DEPTH &WIDTH 90)
A             LIB         10A   P
A             FILE        10A   P
A             MBR         10A   P
A             DOWN         5S  3P
A             ACROSS       5S  3P
A             DEPTH        5S  3P
A             WIDTH        5S  3P
```

HIGHLIGHT (Highlight)

Level	Conditioning	DataStream	Parameters
Record	Yes	SCS	None
Field			

This keyword prints fields in bold letters. When this keyword is used with AFP data streams, the field must be using a registered font ID.

```
....1....+....2....+....3....+....4....+....5....+....6....+....7....+....8
A             R FORMAT1
A               CUSNBR        7S 0   10 10HIGHLIGHT
A               CUSNAM       35A     10 20
```

INDARA (Indicator Area)

Level	Conditioning	DataStream	Parameters
File	No	SCS	None

This keyword sets up a separate 99-byte indicator buffer. INDARA is mainly used by Cobol programs. All indicators used by a record format will be placed into this buffer instead of being sent with the record format.

```
....1....+....2....+....3....+....4....+....5....+....6....+....7....+....8
A                                       INDARA
A             R FORMAT1
A   01          CUSNBR        7S 0   10 10
A               CUSNAM       35A     10 20
```

INDTXT (Indicator Text)

Level	Conditioning	DataStream	Parameters
File	No	SCS	1) Indicator
Record			2) Indicator-text

This keyword documents how an indicator is used. INDTXT serves no other purpose than documentation.

PARAMETER DEFINITIONS

Indicator
This parameter is a number between 1 and 99.

Indicator-text
This parameter is a description up to 50 characters in length enclosed by single quotes (').

```
....1....+....2....+....3....+....4....+....5....+....6....+....7....+....8
A          R FORMAT1
A                                          INDTXT(40 'Print customer #')
A   40         CUSNBR        7S 0  10 10
A              CUSNAM       35A     10 20
```

INVMMAP (Invoke Medium Map)

Level	Conditioning	DataStream	Parameters
Record	Yes	AFPDS	1) Medium-map-name

This keyword is used to invoke a new medium map within a form definition. The medium map lets the user select or change print parameters such as an input drawer, page rotation, or overlays.

PARAMETER DEFINITION

Medium-map-name
This parameter specifies the name of the medium map within the form definition. The name can be defined as a hard-coded value or as a program to system field.

LINE (Line)

Level	Conditioning	DataStream	Parameters
Record	Yes	AFP	1) Position-down
			2) Position-across
			3) Line-direction
			4) Line-width
			5) Line-pad (Optional)

This keyword lets you draw a line on the page. LINE is valid only for AFP data streams.

PARAMETER DEFINITIONS

Position-down
This parameter specifies the vertical starting position of the line to be printed. This is the position down from the top margin of the page. The valid values are 0-22.75 for inches and 0-57.79 for centimeters.

You can also specify this parameter via a variable name. If you do so, that field name must be defined within the same record format, have a data type of S, be five digits in length with three decimal positions, and have a usage of P.

Position-across

This parameter specifies the horizontal starting position of the line to be printed. This is the position across from the left margin of the page. The valid values are 0-22.75 for inches and 0-57.79 for centimeters.

You can also specify this parameter via a variable. To do so, you would use the same rules as for the position-down parameter.

Line-direction

This parameter indicates the direction of the line on the page. The valid values are *HRZ (Horizontal) and *VRT (Vertical).

Line-width

This parameter defines the width of the line to be printed. The valid values are 0-22.75 for inches and 0-57.79 for centimeters. You can also specify a value of *NARROW, *MEDIUM, or *WIDE. *NARROW is a line with a width of .008 in. or .022 cm. *MEDIUM is a line with a width of .017 in. or .042 cm. *WIDE is a line with a width of .025 in. or .064 cm.

Line-pad

This optional parameter indicates whether the line width is to extend beyond the position specified in the position-down and position-across parameters.

The valid values are *TOP and *BOT for horizontal lines. For vertical lines, the valid values are *LEFT and *RIGHT.

```
....1....+....2....+....3....+....4....+....5....+....6....+....7....+....8
A           R FORMAT1
A                                   LINE(0 0 10 *HRZ *NARROW)
```

LPI (Lines Per Inch)

Level	Conditioning	DataStream	Parameters
Record	No	IPDS	1) Lines-per-inch

This keyword sets the lines per inch for printing a record format. LPI may not work as expected with SCS data streams (i.e., the printer must support program-controlled lines per inch). This keyword will override the LPI parameter on the CRTPRTF, CHGPRTF, and OVRPRTF commands.

PARAMETER DEFINITIONS

Lines-per-inch

This parameter is the lines per inch to use when printing. The valid values are 4, 6, 8, 9, and 12.

```
....1....+....2....+....3....+....4....+....5....+....6....+....7....+....8
A          R FORMAT1                    LPI(8)
A            CUSNBR         7S 0   10 10
A            CUSNAM        35A      10 20
```

MSGCON (Message Constant)

Level	Conditioning	DataStream	Parameters
Field	No	SCS	1) Length
			2) Message-ID
			3) Message-file

This keyword prints text on the page where the text is stored in a message file.

PARAMETER DEFINITIONS

Length
This parameter specifies the number of characters to be printed.

Message-ID
This parameter is the seven-character identifier of the message ID that contains the text.

Message-file
This parameter is the name of the message file that contains the message ID. You can optionally specify the library where the message file is found.

```
....1....+....2....+....3....+....4....+....5....+....6....+....7....+....8
A          R FORMAT1
A                                10 10MSGCON(10 USR0001 USERMSGF)
```

OVERLAY (Overlay)

Level	Conditioning	DataStream	Parameters
Record	Yes	AFP	1) Overlay-name
			2) Position-down
			3) Position-across

This keyword prints an overlay image on the page. OVERLAY is valid only for AFP data streams.

PARAMETER DEFINITIONS

Overlay-name
This parameter is the name of the overlay to print. You can optionally specify the library where the overlay is found. You can also use a variable field to

specify the name of the overlay and/or library. If you use a variable field, the field must be defined within the same record format, have a data type of A, and have a usage of P. The length of the field must be 10 if used for a library name and 8 if used for an overlay name.

Position-down

This parameter specifies the vertical starting position of the overlay to be printed. This is the position down from the top of the page margin. The valid values are 0-22.75 for inches and 0-57.79 for centimeters.

You can also specify this parameter via a variable name. If you do so, that field name must be defined within the same record format, have a data type of S, be five digits in length with three decimal positions, and have a usage of P.

Position-across

This parameter specifies the horizontal starting position of the overlay to be printed. This is the position across from the left margin of the page. The valid values are 0-22.75 for inches and 0-57.79 for centimeters.

You can also specify this parameter via a variable. To do so, you would use the same rules as for the position-down parameter.

```
....1....+....2....+....3....+....4....+....5....+....6....+....7....+....8
A          R FORMAT1
A                                     OVERLAY(OVL1 0.5 0.5)
A                                     OVERLAY(&NAME &DOWN &ACROSS)
A            NAME          8A  P
A            DOWN          5S 3P
A            ACROSS        5S 3P
```

PAGNBR (Page Number)

Level	Conditioning	DataStream	Parameters
Field	Yes	SCS	None

This keyword prints the current page number on a page. If you specify a conditioning indicator with this keyword, the page number will still be printed. However, the page number will be reset to 1.

```
....1....+....2....+....3....+....4....+....5....+....6....+....7....+....8
A          R FORMAT1
A                                     1120'Page:'
A                                     1126PAGNBR
```

PAGRTT (Page Rotation)

Level	Conditioning	DataStream	Parameters
Record	Yes	SCS	1) Rotation

This keyword rotates the print on the page for the specified record format. The printer you are using must be able to handle page rotation; for example, a 3812 printer.

PARAMETER DEFINITION

Rotation

This parameter is a value of 0, 90, 180, or 270 that indicates the degree of rotation to be performed.

```
....1....+....2....+....3....+....4....+....5....+....6....+....7....+....8
A           R FORMAT1
A   40                                       PAGRTT(90)
A               CUSNBR        7S 0  10 10
A               CUSNAM        35A    10 20
```

PAGSEG (Page Segment)

Level	Conditioning	DataStream	Parameters
Record	Yes	AFP	1) Page-segment-name
			2) Position-down
			3) Position-across

This keyword prints a page segment. PAGSEG is valid only for AFP data streams.

PARAMETER DEFINITIONS

Page-segment-name

This parameter is the name of the page segment to print. You can optionally specify the library where the page segment is found. You can also use a variable field to specify the name of the page segment and/or library. If you use a variable field, the field must be defined within the same record format, have a data type of A, and have a usage of P. The length of the field must be 10 characters for specifying a library name and 8 characters for specifying a page-segment name.

Position-down

This parameter specifies the vertical starting position of the page segment to be printed. This is the position down from the top of the page margin. The valid values are 0-22.75 for inches and 0-57.79 for centimeters.

You can also specify this parameter via a variable name. If you do so, that field name must be defined within the same record format, have a data type of S, be five digits in length with three decimal positions, and have a usage of P.

Position-across

This parameter specifies the horizontal starting position of the page segment to be printed. This is the position across from the left margin of the page. The valid values are 0-22.75 for inches and 0-57.79 for centimeters.

You can also specify this parameter via a variable. If you do so, you would use the same rules as for the position-down parameter.

```
....1....+....2....+....3....+....4....+....5....+....6....+....7....+....8
A           R FORMAT1
A                                        PAGSEG(PAGE2 0.5 0.5)
A                                        PAGSEG(&NAME &DOWN &ACROSS)
A             NAME          8A   P
A             DOWN          5S  3P
A             ACROSS        5S  3P
```

POSITION (Position)

Level	Conditioning	DataStream	Parameters
Field	Yes	AFP	1) Position-down
			2) Position-across

This keyword lets you print a field at a specific location on a page. POSITION is valid only for AFP data streams. You cannot specify the location (columns 39-44) when using this keyword.

PARAMETER DEFINITIONS

Position-down

This parameter specifies the vertical starting position of the field to be printed. This is the position down from the top of the page margin. The valid values are 0-22.75 for inches and 0-57.79 for centimeters.

You can also specify this parameter via a variable name. If you do so, that field name must be defined within the same record format, have a data type of S, be five digits in length with three decimal positions, and have a usage of P.

Position-across

This parameter specifies the horizontal starting position of the field to be printed. This is the position across from the left margin of the page. The valid values are 0-22.75 for inches and 0-57.79 for centimeters.

You can also specify this parameter via a variable. If you do so, you would use the same rules as for the position-down parameter.

```
....1....+....2....+....3....+....4....+....5....+....6....+....7....+....8
A           R FORMAT1
A             DOWN          5S  3P
A             ACROSS        5S  3P
A             CUSNBR        7S   0    POSITION(0.5 0.5)
A             CUSNAM        35A       POSITION(&DOWN &ACROSS)
```

PRTQLTY (Print Quality)

Level	Conditioning	DataStream	Parameters
Record	Yes	IPDS	1) Print-quality
Field			

This keyword defines the print quality for a field or record format. PRTQLTY must be used in connection with the CHRSIZ or BARCODE keywords.

PARAMETER DEFINITION

Print-quality
The valid values for this parameter are *STD (Standard quality), *DRAFT (Draft quality), *NLQ (Near letter quality), and *FASTDRAFT (Fast draft quality).

```
....1....+....2....+....3....+....4....+....5....+....6....+....7....+....8
A          R FORMAT1
A            CUSNBR       7S 0  10 10CHRSIZ(2 2)
A                                    PRTQLTY(*DRAFT)
```

REF (Reference)

Level	Conditioning	Parameters
File	No	1) File-name
		2) Record-format-name (Optional)

This keyword is used to specify the name of a file from which all field references are to be retrieved. A field is referenced when an R is placed in column 29.

PARAMETER DEFINITIONS

File-name
This parameter is the name of the file from which references can be retrieved. You can optionally specify the library name where the file can be found.

Record-format-name
This optional parameter specifies the particular record format within the file to use for field references.

```
....1....+....2....+....3....+....4....+....5....+....6....+....7....+....8
A                                    REF(REFFILE)
A          R FORMAT1
A            CUSNBR     R        10 10
A            CUSNAM     R        10 20
A            CUSAD1        35A   11 20
....1....+....2....+....3....+....4....+....5....+....6....+....7....+....8
A                                    REF(PRODLIB/REFFILE REFFMT1)
A          R FORMAT1
```

```
....1....+....2....+....3....+....4....+....5....+....6....+....7....+....8
A              CUSNBR    R            10 10
A              CUSNAM    R            10 20
A              CUSAD1          35A    11 20
```

REFFLD (Referenced Field)

Level	Conditioning	Parameters
Field	No	1) Field-name
		2) File-name (Optional)

This keyword lets you retrieve the field reference from another field in a file other than that specified in the REF keyword.

PARAMETER DEFINITIONS

Field-name

This parameter is the name of the field to reference in the other file. You can optionally specify the record-format name where the field is found when the file specified has more than one record format.

File-name

This parameter is the name of the file from which the field reference is to be retrieved. You can specify either the file name or a value of *SRC.*SRC indicates that the field reference exists within this same DDS source. If you don't specify a file name, *SRC is the default. You can optionally specify the library name where the file is found.

```
....1....+....2....+....3....+....4....+....5....+....6....+....7....+....8
A                                          REF(REFFILE)
A          R FORMAT1
A            PART#    R            10 10
A            ITEM           10A    11 10
A            ITEM1    R            12 10REFFLD(ITEM)
A            ITEM2    R            13 10REFFLD(FORMAT1/ITEM)
A            ITEM3    R            14 10REFFLD(ITEM *SRC)
A            ITEM4    R            15 10REFFLD(ITEM FILE2)
A            ITEM5    R            16 10REFFLD(ITEM PRODLIB/FILE2)
```

SKIPA (Skip After)

Level	Conditioning	DataStream	Parameters
File	Yes	SCS	1) Line-number
Record			
Field			

This keyword lets you skip to a specific line after printing information on the page. You must use conditioning indicators when SKIPA is specified at the file level. This keyword is not valid at the file level for AFP data streams.

You cannot specify line numbers (columns 39-41) when using this keyword.

PARAMETER DEFINITION

Line-number

This parameter is the line number to skip to after printing. The valid range is 1 to 255.

```
....1....+....2....+....3....+....4....+....5....+....6....+....7....+....8
A          R FORMAT1
A            CUSNBR       7S 0      10
A            CUSNAM       35A       20SKIPA(15)
```

SKIPB (Skip Before)

Level	Conditioning	DataStream	Parameters
File	Yes	SCS	1) Line-number
Record			
Field			

This keyword lets you skip to a specific line number before printing information on the page. You must use conditioning indicators when SKIPB is specified at the file level. This keyword is not valid at the file level for AFP data streams.

You cannot specify line numbers (columns 39-41) when using this keyword.

PARAMETER DEFINITION

Line-number

This parameter is the line number to skip to before printing. The valid range is 1 to 255.

```
....1....+....2....+....3....+....4....+....5....+....6....+....7....+....8
A          R FORMAT1                        SKIPB(10)
A            CUSNBR       7S 0      10
A            CUSNAM       35A       20
```

SPACEA (Space After)

Level	Conditioning	DataStream	Parameters
Record	Yes	SCS	1) Space-value
Field			

This keyword lets you skip a specific number of lines on the page after printing information on the page.

You cannot specify line numbers (columns 39-41) when using this keyword.

PARAMETER DEFINITION

Space-value

This parameter is a number between 0 and 255

```
....1....+....2....+....3....+....4....+....5....+....6....+....7....+....8
A              R FORMAT1
A                CUSNBR       7S 0      10
A                CUSNAM       35A       20SPACEA(3)
```

SPACEB (Space Before)

Level	Conditioning	DataStream	Parameters
Record	Yes	SCS	1) Space-value
Field			

This keyword lets you skip a specific number of lines on the page before information is printed on the page.

You cannot specify line numbers (columns 39-41) when using this keyword.

PARAMETER DEFINITION

Space-value

This parameter is a number between 0 and 255.

```
....1....+....2....+....3....+....4....+....5....+....6....+....7....+....8
A              R FORMAT1
A                CUSNBR       7S 0      10SPACEB(2)
A                CUSNAM       35A       20
```

TEXT (Text)

Level	Conditioning	DataStream	Parameters
Record	No	SCS	1) Description
Field			

This keyword lets you add descriptive text to record formats or fields. This text serves as documentation only.

PARAMETER DEFINITION

Description

This parameter is a text field up to 50 characters in length enclosed in single quotes.

```
....1....+....2....+....3....+....4....+....5....+....6....+....7....+....8
A              R FORMAT1
A                CUSNBR        7S 0   10 10TEXT('Customer #')
A                CUSNAM        35A    10 20
```

TIME (Time)

Level	Conditioning	DataStream	Parameters
Field	No	SCS	None

This keyword prints the current system time on a page.

```
....1....+....2....+....3....+....4....+....5....+....6....+....7....+....8
A              R FORMAT1
A                                      1  2'Time:'
A                                      1  8TIME
```

TIMFMT (Time Format)

Level	Conditioning	DataStream	Parameters
Field	No	SCS	1) Time-format

This keyword defines the time format for a time field.

PARAMETER DEFINITION

Time-format

This parameter is a code that represents the format of a time field.

Code	Meaning	Format
*HMS	Hours:Minutes:Seconds	hh:mm:ss
*ISO	International Standards Organization	hh.mm.ss
*USA	USA Standard	hh:mm AM or hh:mm PM
*EUR	European Standard	hh.mm.ss
*JIS	Japanese Standard	hh:mm:ss

```
....1....+....2....+....3....+....4....+....5....+....6....+....7....+....8
A              R FORMAT1
A                TIMFLD1       T     10 10TIMFMT(*ISO)
A                TIMFLD2       T     12 10TIMFMT(*USA)
A                TIMFLD3       T     14 10TIMFMT(*HMS)
```

TIMSEP (Time Separator)

Level	Conditioning	DataStream	Parameters
Field	No	SCS	1) Time-separator

This keyword overrides the time separator for the printer file time field.

PARAMETER DEFINITION

Time-separator
This parameter is either an explicit value defined within single quotes (') or a
value of *JOB. The valid values are colon (:), period (.), or blank ( ). *JOB
indicates you are to use the default found for the job.

```
....1....+....2....+....3....+....4....+....5....+....6....+....7....+....8
A          R FORMAT1
A            TIMFLD1         T     10 10TIMFMT(*ISO)
A            TIMFLD2         T     12 10TIMFMT(*USA)
A            TIMFLD3         T     14 10TIMFMT(*HMS)
A                                     TIMSEP(':')
```

TRNSPY (Transparency)

Level	Conditioning	DataStream	Parameters
Field	No	SCS	None

You use this keyword in connection with the DFNCHR and CVTDTA keywords
to prevent an SCS printer from interpreting the data stream as printer control
codes. This keyword is used only for SCS printers.

```
....1....+....2....+....3....+....4....+....5....+....6....+....7....+....8
A          R FORMAT1                    DFNCHR(x'51' 'FF00FF00FF00FF00FF')
A            FIELD1          10A     10 20CVTDTA
A                                       TRNSPY
```

TXTRTT (Text Rotation)

Level	Conditioning	DataStream	Parameters
Field	Yes	AFP	1) Rotation

This keyword rotates the text in a field on the page. TXTRTT is valid only for
AFP data streams.

PARAMETER DEFINITION

Rotation
The valid values for this parameter are 0, 90, 180, or 270. The specified value
indicates the degree of rotation to take place.

```
....1....+....2....+....3....+....4....+....5....+....6....+....7....+....8
A          R FORMAT1
A            CUSNBR       7S 0  10 10TXTRTT(90)
A            CUSNAM      35A     10 20
```

UNDERLINE (Underline)

Level	Conditioning	DataStream	Parameters
Field	Yes	SCS	None

This keyword prints an underline for the field when it is printed.

```
....1....+....2....+....3....+....4....+....5....+....6....+....7....+....8
A          R FORMAT1
A            CUSNBR       7S 0  10 10UNDERLINE
A            CUSNAM      35A     10 20
```

Chapter 5

Intersystem Communications Function (ICF) Files

You use ICF files to communicate information between two different computer systems running over some type of communications network. This means that two programs, one on each machine, are talking to each other, passing data back and forth.

This section discusses the keywords you might use when writing an ICF application; it does not explain how to code ICF programs.

DATA TYPES

The following table shows the valid data types (column 35) for ICF files:

Code	Meaning
P	Packed decimal
S	Zoned decimal
B	Binary
F	Floating point
A	Character

If you don't specify a data type, the default will be A for character fields and S for numeric fields.

FIELD USAGE

The following table shows what field usages (column 38) are available for ICF files:

Code	Meaning
blank	Both input and output
B	Both input and output
P	Program-to-system field

KEYWORD LEVELS

ICF files have three distinct levels for which keywords can be specified. These are file level, record-format level, and field level.

File level refers to those keywords that will affect the entire ICF file. The keywords are placed before the first record format in the DDS source.

Record-format level refers to those keywords that affect the format of the ICF file. You define a record format by placing an R in column 17 of the A-spec. You place these keywords before the first field definition in the record format.

Field level refers to those keywords that affect an individual field within the record format.

KEYWORDS

The column "Conditioning" in the tables indicates whether you are allowed to specify indicators in columns 7 through 16. Typically, you will use conditioning indicators for keywords when they are specified at the file level.

ALIAS (Alternative Name)

Level	Conditioning	Parameters
Field	No	1) Alternate-name

This keyword lets you assign a name longer than 10 characters for a field. If your HLL program (e.g., Cobol, PL/1) supports longer field names, this alias definition will be used; otherwise, it is ignored.

PARAMETER DEFINITION

Alternate-name

The alternate name specified for this parameter can be up to 30 characters in length.

```
....1....+....2....+....3....+....4....+....5....+....6....+....7....+....8
A          R FORMAT1
A            CUSNBR        7P 0       ALIAS(CUSTOMER_NUMBER)
A            CUSNAM        35A        ALIAS(CUSTOMER_NAME)
```

ALWWRT (Allow Write)

Level	Conditioning	Parameters
File	Yes	None
Record		

You use this keyword to allow your program to notify the receiving program that you are done sending information to that program. This operation allows the other program to send data back.

```
....1....+....2....+....3....+....4....+....5....+....6....+....7....+....8
A   40                                          ALWWRT
A          R FORMAT1
A            CUSNBR        7P 0
A            CUSNAM        35A
```

CANCEL (Cancel)

Level	Conditioning	Parameters
File	Yes	None
Record		

You use this keyword to cancel the current group of records being sent to the remote program.

```
....1....+....2....+....3....+....4....+....5....+....6....+....7....+....8
A  40                                      CANCEL
A            R FORMAT1
A              CUSNBR        7P 0
A              CUSNAM       35A
```

CNLINVITE (Cancel Invite)

Level	Conditioning	Parameters
File	Yes	None
Record		

You use this keyword to cancel an invite request when no input data has yet been received from the remote program.

```
....1....+....2....+....3....+....4....+....5....+....6....+....7....+....8
A            R FORMAT1            CNLINVITE
```

CONFIRM (Confirm)

Level	Conditioning	Parameters
File	Yes	None
Record		

You use this keyword to request that the remote program send a confirmation that it received the data you have sent. This keyword will work only if SYNLVL(*CONFIRM) was specified on the send data request.

```
....1....+....2....+....3....+....4....+....5....+....6....+....7....+....8
A            R FORMAT1
A  40                             CONFIRM
```

CTLDTA (Control Data)

Level	Conditioning	Parameters
File	Yes	None
Record		

You use this keyword to tell the remote program that you are sending control data.

```
....1....+....2....+....3....+....4....+....5....+....6....+....7....+....8
A            R FORMAT1                     CTLDTA
A              DATA          100A
```

DETACH (Detach)

Level	Conditioning	Parameters
File	Yes	None
Record		

You use this keyword to inform the remote program that you are done sending data and that you wish to end sending data for the present time. You must issue another EVOKE keyword for your program to send more data after a DETACH has been issued.

```
....1....+....2....+....3....+....4....+....5....+....6....+....7....+....8
A            R FORMAT1
A   40                                    DETACH
```

DFREVOKE (Defer Evoke)

Level	Conditioning	Parameters
File	Yes	None
Record		

You use this keyword in connection with the EVOKE keyword to defer the evoke request until the send buffer is full of data, or until a FRCDTA keyword is issued.

```
....1....+....2....+....3....+....4....+....5....+....6....+....7....+....8
A            R FORMAT1
A                                    EVOKE(REMOTEPGM)
A                                    DFREVOKE
```

ENDGRP (End Group)

Level	Conditioning	Parameters
File	Yes	None
Record		

You use this keyword to signal the end of a user-defined group of records.

```
....1....+....2....+....3....+....4....+....5....+....6....+....7....+....8
A          R FORMAT1                    ENDGRP
```

EOS (End of Session)

Level	Conditioning	Parameters
File	Yes	None
Record		

You use this keyword to release communications with the remote system. This action is the equivalent of closing the ICF file.

```
....1....+....2....+....3....+....4....+....5....+....6....+....7....+....8
A  40                                   EOS
A          R FORMAT1
```

EVOKE (Evoke)

Level	Conditioning	Parameters
File	Yes	1) Program-name
Record		2) Parameters (Optional)

You use this keyword to indicate the name of the program to execute on the remote system. By issuing this keyword, you are starting the specified program on the remote system. You would then send and receive data with that program.

PARAMETER DEFINITIONS

Program-name
This parameter is the name of the program on the remote system. You can either hard-code the program name or use a variable field. If you use a variable field, that field must be defined within the record format as a character field (data type A).

You can optionally specify the library name where the remote program resides. You can also use a variable name just like the program name for the library.

Parameters
You can specify up to 255 parameters that will be passed to the remote program when it is started. Doing this would have the same effect as if you called the program using the CALL command. You can pass either character or numeric data. You can also use variable names to pass parameter data.

```
....1....+....2....+....3....+....4....+....5....+....6....+....7....+....8
A              R FORMAT1
A  40                                          EVOKE(REMOTEPGM1)
A  41                                          EVOKE(REMOTEPGM2 'HI')
A  42                                          EVOKE(&LIB/&PGM 'HI')
A  43                                          EVOKE(REMOTEPGM3 &PARM1 &PARM2)
A              LIB            10A  P
A              PGM            10A  P
A              PARM1           2A  P
A              PARM2           6A  P
```

FAIL (Fail)

Level	Conditioning	Parameters
File	Yes	None
Record		

You use this keyword to inform the remote program that the data it received was invalid.

```
....1....+....2....+....3....+....4....+....5....+....6....+....7....+....8
A              R FORMAT1                        FAIL
```

FLTPCN (Floating-Point Precision)

Level	Conditioning	Parameters
Field	No	1) Precision

You use this keyword to define the precision of a floating-point field (data type F).

PARAMETER DEFINITION

Precision

This parameter is a value of either *SINGLE or *DOUBLE. Single-precision fields can be up to 9 digits long, whereas double-precision fields can be up to 17 digits long. If you don't specify this keyword, the default is single precision.

```
....1....+....2....+....3....+....4....+....5....+....6....+....7....+....8
A              R FORMAT1
A              CALC1          17F  5           FLTPCN(*DOUBLE)
A              CALC2           8F  3           FLTPCN(*SINGLE)
A              CALC3           8F  2
```

FMH (Function Management Header)

Level	Conditioning	Parameters
File	Yes	None
Record		

You use this keyword to inform the remote program that you are sending a function management header (FMH).

```
....1....+....2....+....3....+....4....+....5....+....6....+....7....+....8
A          R FORMAT1              FMH
A            FMHDTA      10A  B
```

FMTNAME (Format Name)

Level	Conditioning	Parameters
File	Yes	None
Record		

You use this keyword to send the record format name to the remote program when your program issues an output operation.

```
....1....+....2....+....3....+....4....+....5....+....6....+....7....+....8
A          R FORMAT1                    FMTNAME
```

INDARA (Indicator Area)

Level	Conditioning	Parameters
File	No	None

You use this keyword to separate all indicators into a separate input/output buffer. INDARA is used mainly by COBOL/400 programs to simplify the programming requirements for handling indicators, although any programming language supports this feature. The input/output buffer is 99 bytes long.

```
....1....+....2....+....3....+....4....+....5....+....6....+....7....+....8
A                                    INDARA
A          R FORMAT1
```

INDTXT (Indicator Text)

Level	Conditioning	Parameters
File	No	1) Indicator
Record		2) Indicator-text

This keyword lets you specify documentation for how indicators are used in the DDS source file. INDTXT serves no other purpose than documentation.

PARAMETER DEFINITIONS

Indicator
This parameter is a number between 1 and 99.

Indicator-text

This parameter is a text description up to 50 characters in length embedded in single quotes (').

```
....1....+....2....+....3....+....4....+....5....+....6....+....7....+....8
A                                               INDTXT(40 'Shut down program')
A   40                                          EOS
A              R FORMAT1
A
A                                               INDTXT(41 'Start remote program')
A   41                                          EVOKE(REMOTEPGM1)
```

INVITE (Invite)

Level	Conditioning	Parameters
File	Yes	None
Record		

This keyword prepares your HLL program to receive data from the remote program. You issue an output operation (using a write operation) with the INVITE keyword active, which allows the remote program to "send" you data while your program continues to do other work. Then when you want to receive the data, you issue your read request. You use this keyword mainly to improve performance.

```
....1....+....2....+....3....+....4....+....5....+....6....+....7....+....8
A   40                                          INVITE
A              R FORMAT1
A                 CUSNBR        7P 0
A                 CUSNAM        35A
```

NEGRSP (Negative Response)

Level	Conditioning	Parameters
File	Yes	1) Field-name (Optional)
Record		

You use this keyword to send a "negative" response to the remote program. NEGRSP is used mainly to indicate an error condition in the data that was received from the remote program.

PARAMETER DEFINITION

Field-name

This optional parameter is a field name that contains the sense data to be sent to the remote program. The field name must be defined in the record format, be a character (data type A), have a minimum length of eight characters, and have a usage of B (Both). The use of a field name is not allowed at the file level.

```
....1....+....2....+....3....+....4....+....5....+....6....+....7....+....8
A           R FORMAT1
A   40                               NEGRSP(&SENSE)
A           SENSE         10A  B
```

PRPCMT (Prepare for Commit)

Level	Conditioning	Parameters
Record	Yes	None

You use this keyword to inform the remote program that it is to get ready for a synchronization point. Any data in the buffer will be sent to the remote program when this keyword is issued. PRPCMT is valid only when SYNLVL(*COMMIT) is also used.

```
....1....+....2....+....3....+....4....+....5....+....6....+....7....+....8
A           R FORMAT1
A                                   PRPCMT
```

RCVCANCEL (Receive Cancel)

Level	Conditioning	Parameters
File	No	1) Response-indicator
Record		2) Text (Optional)

This keyword specifies that a response-indicator is to be turned on when your program receives a CANCEL request from the remote program.

PARAMETER DEFINITIONS

Response-indicator
This parameter is a value between 01 and 99 that represents the indicator to be turned on.

Text
This optional parameter lets you define documentation text up to 50 characters in length. The text must be enclosed in single quotes (').

```
....1....+....2....+....3....+....4....+....5....+....6....+....7....+....8
A                                   RCVCANCEL(55 'Cancel request')
A           R FORMAT1
```

RCVCONFIRM (Receive Confirm)

Level	Conditioning	Parameters
File	No	1) Response-indicator
Record		2) Text (Optional)

This keyword specifies that a response-indicator is to be turned on when your program receives a CONFIRM request from the remote program.

PARAMETER DEFINITIONS

Response-indicator

This parameter is a value between 01 and 99 that represents the indicator to be turned on.

Text

This optional parameter lets you define documentation text up to 50 characters in length. The text must be enclosed in single quotes (').

```
....1....+....2....+....3....+....4....+....5....+....6....+....7....+....8
A                                            RCVCONFIRM(56 'Confirmation request-
A                                            ed')
A          R FORMAT1
```

RCVCTLDTA (Receive Control Data)

Level	Conditioning	Parameters
File	No	1) Response-indicator
Record		2) Text (Optional)

This keyword specifies that a response-indicator is to be turned on when your program receives control data (CTLDTA) from the remote program.

PARAMETER DEFINITIONS

Response-indicator

This parameter is a value between 01 and 99 that represents the indicator to be turned on.

Text

This optional parameter lets you define documentation text up to 50 characters in length. The text must be enclosed in single quotes (').

```
....1....+....2....+....3....+....4....+....5....+....6....+....7....+....8
A                                            RCVCTLDTA(57 'Control data receive-
A                                            d')
A          R FORMAT1
```

RCVDETACH (Receive Detach)

Level	Conditioning	Parameters
File	No	1) Response-indicator
Record		2) Text (Optional)

This keyword specifies that a response-indicator is to be turned on when your program receives a DETACH request from the remote program.

PARAMETER DEFINITIONS

Response-indicator
This parameter is a value between 01 and 99 that represents the indicator to be turned on.

Text
This optional parameter lets you define documentation text up to 50 characters in length. The text must be enclosed in single quotes (').

```
....1....+....2....+....3....+....4....+....5....+....6....+....7....+....8
A                                  RCVDETACH(58 'Detach request')
A            R FORMAT1
```

RCVENDGRP (Receive End of Group)

Level	Conditioning	Parameters
File	No	1) Response-indicator
Record		2) Text (Optional)

This keyword specifies that a response-indicator is to be turned on when your program receives an End of Group (ENDGRP) notification from the remote program.

PARAMETER DEFINITIONS

Response-indicator
This parameter is a value between 01 and 99 that represents the indicator to be turned on.

Text
This optional parameter lets you define documentation text up to 50 characters in length. The text must be enclosed in single quotes (').

```
....1....+....2....+....3....+....4....+....5....+....6....+....7....+....8
A                                  RCVENDGRP(59 'End of Group received-
A                                  ')
A            R FORMAT1
```

RCVFAIL (Receive Fail)

Level	Conditioning	Parameters
File	No	1) Response-indicator
Record		2) Text (Optional)

This keyword specifies that a response-indicator is to be turned on when your program receives a FAIL notification from the remote program.

PARAMETER DEFINITIONS

Response-indicator
This parameter is a value between 01 and 99 that represents the indicator to be turned on.

Text
This optional parameter lets you define documentation text up to 50 characters in length. The text must be enclosed in single quotes (').

```
....1....+....2....+....3....+....4....+....5....+....6....+....7....+....8
A                                         RCVFAIL(60 'Fail received')
A          R FORMAT1
```

RCVFMH (Receive Function Management Header)

Level	Conditioning	Parameters
File	No	1) Response-indicator
Record		2) Text (Optional)

This keyword specifies that a response-indicator is to be turned on when your program receives a Function Management Header (FMH) from the remote program.

PARAMETER DEFINITIONS

Response-indicator
This parameter is a value between 01 and 99 that represents the indicator to be turned on.

Text
This optional parameter lets you define documentation text up to 50 characters in length. The text must be enclosed in single quotes (').

```
....1....+....2....+....3....+....4....+....5....+....6....+....7....+....8
A                                         RCVFMH(61 'Function Management Head-
A                                         er received')
A          R FORMAT1
```

RCVNEGRSP (Receive Negative Response)

Level	Conditioning	Parameters
File	No	1) Response-indicator
Record		2) Text (Optional)

This keyword specifies that a response-indicator is to be turned on when your program receives a Negative Response (NEGRSP) from the remote program.

PARAMETER DEFINITIONS

Response-indicator
This parameter is a value between 01 and 99 that represents the indicator to be turned on.

Text
This optional parameter lets you define documentation text up to 50 characters in length. The text must be enclosed in single quotes (').

```
....1....+....2....+....3....+....4....+....5....+....6....+....7....+....8
A                                      RCVNEGRSP(62 'Negative Response -
A                                      received')
A          R FORMAT1
```

RCVROLLB (Receive Rollback)

Level	Conditioning	Parameters
File	No	1) Response-indicator
Record		2) Text (Optional)

This keyword specifies that a response indicator is to be turned on when your program receives a rollback operation request from the remote program.

PARAMETER DEFINITIONS

Response-indicator
This parameter is a value between 01 and 99 that represents the indicator to be turned on.

Text
This optional parameter lets you define documentation text up to 50 characters in length. The text must be enclosed in single quotes (').

```
....1....+....2....+....3....+....4....+....5....+....6....+....7....+....8
A                                      RCVROLLB(63 'Rollback received')
A          R FORMAT1
```

RCVTKCMT (Receive Take Commit)

Level	Conditioning	Parameters
File	No	1) Response-indicator
		2) Text (Optional)

This keyword specifies that a response indicator is to be turned on when your program receives a take commit request from the remote program (see the PRPCMT keyword).

PARAMETER DEFINITIONS

Response-indicator

This parameter is a value between 01 and 99 that represents the indicator to be turned on.

Text

This optional parameter lets you define documentation text up to 50 characters in length. The text must be enclosed in single quotes (').

```
....1....+....2....+....3....+....4....+....5....+....6....+....7....+....8
A                                       RCVTKCMT(64 'Take commit received')
A          R FORMAT1
```

RCVTRNRND (Receive Turnaround)

Level	Conditioning	Parameters
File	No	1) Response-indicator
Record		2) Text (Optional)

This keyword specifies that a response-indicator is to be turned on when your program receives a notice that the remote program has finished sending data (ALWWRT) and your program can now send data.

PARAMETER DEFINITIONS

Response-indicator

This parameter is a value between 01 and 99 that represents the indicator to be turned on.

Text

This optional parameter lets you define documentation text up to 50 characters in length. The text must be enclosed in single quotes (').

```
....1....+....2....+....3....+....4....+....5....+....6....+....7....+....8
A                                       RCVRTRNRND(65 'Turnaround received')
A          R FORMAT1
```

RECID (Record Identification)

Level	Conditioning	Parameters
Record	No	1) Starting-position
		2) Compare-value

The RECID keyword is used to identify which record format was received from the remote program. This keyword is needed because you issue read requests against the ICF file name, not the record-format name. Both your program and the remote program must agree on how this identification will take place.

The data received will be mapped to the record format identified. You must remember to specify FMTSLT(*RECID) on the ADDICFDEVE, CHGICFDEVE, or OVRICFDEVE commands for this keyword to be used.

PARAMETER DEFINITIONS

Starting-position

This parameter is a number that indicates where in the data buffer the starting position of the identifying characters is located. You can either specify a number or *POSnnnnn, where *nnnnn* is the number; the meanings are the same.

Compare-value

This parameter is the character string that will be tested. You can specify *ZERO, *BLANK, or a character string enclosed in single quotes ('). *ZERO indicates the character must be a '0'. *BLANKS indicates the character must be a ' '.

```
....1....+....2....+....3....+....4....+....5....+....6....+....7....+....8
A           R FORMAT1                    RECID(1 'H')
A             HDDATA        10A
  *
A           R FORMAT2                    RECID(*POS1 'D')
A             CUSNBR         7P 0
A             CUSNAM        35A
  *
A           R FORMAT3                    RECID(1 'T')
A             TOTAL          9P 0
```

REF (Reference)

Level	Conditioning	Parameters
File	No	1) File-name
		2) Record-format-name (Optional)

You use this keyword to specify the name of a file from which all field references are to be retrieved. A field is referenced when you place an R in column 29.

PARAMETER DEFINITIONS

File-name

This parameter is the name of the file from which references can be retrieved. You can optionally specify the library name where the file can be found.

Record-format-name

This optional parameter specifies the specific record format within the file to use for field references.

```
....1....+....2....+....3....+....4....+....5....+....6....+....7....+....8
A                                              REF(REFFILE)
A          R FORMAT1
A            CUSNBR      R
A            CUSNAM      R
A            CUSAD1         35A
```

```
....1....+....2....+....3....+....4....+....5....+....6....+....7....+....8
A                                              REF(PRODLIB/REFFILE REFFMT1)
A          R FORMAT1
A            CUSNBR      R
A            CUSNAM      R
A            CUSAD1         35A
```

REFFLD (Referenced Field)

Level	Conditioning	Parameters
Field	No	1) Field-name
		2) File-name (Optional)

You use this keyword to retrieve the field reference from another field in a file other than that specified in the REF keyword.

PARAMETER DEFINITIONS

Field-name

This parameter is the name of the field to reference in the other file. You can optionally specify the record-format name where the field is found when the file specified has more than one record format.

File-name

This parameter is the name of the file from which the field reference is to be retrieved. You can specify either the file name or a value of *SRC. *SRC indicates that the field reference exists within the same DDS source. If you don't specify a file name, *SRC is the default. You can optionally specify the library name where the file is found.

```
....1....+....2....+....3....+....4....+....5....+....6....+....7....+....8
A                                          REF(REFFILE)
A          R FORMAT1
A            PART#     R
A            ITEM             10A
A            ITEM1     R      REFFLD(ITEM)
A            ITEM2     R      REFFLD(FORMAT1/ITEM)
A            ITEM3     R      REFFLD(ITEM *SRC)
A            ITEM4     R      REFFLD(ITEM FILE2)
A            ITEM5     R      REFFLD(ITEM PRODLIB/FILE2)
```

RQSWRT (Request Write)

Level	Conditioning	Parameters
File	Yes	None
Record		

You use this keyword to request permission to send data to the remote program.

```
....1....+....2....+....3....+....4....+....5....+....6....+....7....+....8
A          R FORMAT1
A  40                          RQSWRT
```

RSPCONFIRM (Respond Confirm)

Level	Conditioning	Parameters
File	Yes	None
Record		

You use this keyword to send a positive response to a confirmation (CON-FIRM) request from the remote program.

```
....1....+....2....+....3....+....4....+....5....+....6....+....7....+....8
A          R FORMAT1
A  40                          RSPCONFIRM
```

SECURITY (Security)

Level	Conditioning	Parameters
File	Yes	1) Security-subfield
Record		2) Subfield-definition

This keyword lets you include security information when you EVOKE a program on the remote system. Obviously, you must use this keyword in conjunction with the EVOKE keyword.

NOTE: You can specify up to three groups (using both parameters) of security values.

PARAMETER DEFINITIONS

Security-subfield

This parameter is a number between 1 and 3 that indicates what security data is going to be passed to the remote system.

The following table shows the valid values for this parameter and their meanings:

Value	Meaning
1	Profile ID
2	Password
3	User ID

Subfield-definition

This parameter is the actual security value that is to be sent to the remote system. You can specify *USER, *NONE, a character string enclosed in single quotes, or a field name.

*USER indicates the current AS/400 user profile is to be passed to the remote system.

*NONE indicates a null value is to be sent to the remote system.

You can hard-code the value within single quotes (').

You can specify a field name. This field name must not exceed 10 characters in length and must be defined within the same record format.

```
....1....+....2....+....3....+....4....+....5....+....6....+....7....+....8
A                R FORMAT1
A    40                                      SECURITY(2 'NEWS' 3 'USER')
A    40                                      EVOKE(REMOTEPGM1)
*
A    41                                      SECURITY(2 &PASS 3 &USER)
A    41                                      EVOKE(REMOTEPGM2)
*
A                  PASS        10A
A                  USER        10A
```

SUBDEV (Subdevice)

Level	Conditioning	Parameters
File	Yes	1) Device-identifier
Record		

This keyword lets you select a specific subdevice, such as a printer, at the remote system to which you wish to send data.

PARAMETER DEFINITION

Device-identifier

This parameter is a value of *DC1, *DC2, *DC3, or *DC4. You can specify up to four SUBDEV keywords, but you cannot specify the same subdevice at both the file and record-format levels.

```
....1....+....2....+....3....+....4....+....5....+....6....+....7....+....8
A   40                                  SUBDEV(*DC1)
A           R FORMAT1
A   41                                  SUBDEV(*DC2)
A             CUSNBR        7P 0
A             CUSNAM       35A
```

SYNLVL (Synchronization Level)

Level	Conditioning	Parameters
File	Yes	1) Sync-type (Optional)
Record		

You use this keyword to set the synchronization requirements with the remote program at the time it is evoked (EVOKE keyword). Obviously, you must use this keyword in connection with the EVOKE keyword.

PARAMETER DEFINITION

Sync-type

This optional parameter specifies the level of synchronization required. The valid values are *NONE, *CONFIRM, and *COMMIT.

*NONE indicates that neither program will use the CONFIRM keyword; this is the default.

*CONFIRM indicates that you must use the CONFIRM keyword when sending data and the remote program must acknowledge the receipt with either a positive (RSPCONFIRM) or a negative (NEGRSP) response.

*COMMIT indicates that you will be using the PRPCMT keyword together with the appropriate commit and rollback operations.

```
....1....+....2....+....3....+....4....+....5....+....6....+....7....+....8
A           R FORMAT1
A                                       SYNLVL(*CONFIRM)
A                                       EVOKE(REMOTEPGM1)
```

TEXT (Text)

Level	Conditioning	Parameters
Record	No	1) Description
Field		

You use this keyword to add descriptive text to record formats or fields. This text serves as documentation only.

PARAMETER DEFINITION

Description

This parameter is a text field up to 50 characters in length enclosed in single quotes (').

```
....1....+....2...s.+....3....+....4....+....5....+....6....+....7....+...8
A          R FORMAT1                       TEXT('Sales record format')
A            CUSNBR         7P 0            TEXT('Customer number')
A            CUSNAM         35A             TEXT('Customer name')
```

TIMER (Timer)

Level	Conditioning	Parameters
Record	No	1) Time-value

This keyword lets you specify a particular amount of time that your program is to wait for an operation before a time-out return code is issued.

This keyword cannot be issued at the same time as the majority of the keywords available for ICF files. TIMER is used primarily during the sending and receiving of data record formats.

PARAMETER DEFINITION

Time-value

This parameter is the amount of time in hours, minutes, and seconds that the system is to wait until a time-out occurs. The value would be in *HHMMSS* format.

This value can be entered as either a hard-coded value or by means of a variable. If you are using a variable, the field must be defined within the same record format, have a data type of S, be 6 digits in length with zero decimals, and have a usage of P.

```
....1....+....2....+....3....+....4....+....5....+....6....+....7....+....8
A          R FORMAT1                   TIMER(003000)
  *
A          R FORMAT2                   TIMER(&HMS)
A            HMS            6S 0P
A            CUSNBR         7P 0
A            CUSNAM         35A
```

TNSSYNLVL (Transaction Synchronization Level)

Level	Conditioning	Parameters
File	No	None
Record		

You use this keyword to send the synchronization level specified in the SYNLVL keyword to the remote program when you issue either a DETACH or an ALWWRT signal. You must specify this keyword in the same record format as the DETACH or ALWWRT keywords. This prevents the action requested from taking place until a CONFIRM or commit operation is completed by the remote program.

```
....1....+....2....+....3....+....4....+....5....+....6....+....7....+....8
A          R FORMAT1               SYNLVL(*CONFIRM)
A                                  EVOKE(REMOTEPGM1)
A          R FORMAT2
A                                  TNSSYNLVL
A                                  DETACH
```

VARBUFMGT (Variable Buffer Management)

Level	Conditioning	Parameters
Record	No	None

You use this keyword to allow the sending or receiving of multiple or partial records using a single record format.

You would use this keyword along with VARLEN when sending variable records to the remote program. VARLEN is not needed when receiving records from the remote program.

```
....1....+....2....+....3....+....4....+....5....+....6....+....7....+....8
A          R FORMAT1               VARBUFMGT
A            DATA          40A
 *
A          R FORMAT2               VARBUFMGT
A                                  VARLEN(&LEN)
A            LEN           5S 0P
A            DATA          40A
```

VARLEN (Variable Length Data)

Level	Conditioning	Parameters
Record	No	1) Field-name

You use this keyword to send variable length data to a remote program. This keyword is valid on output operations only.

PARAMETER DEFINITION

Field-name

This parameter is the name of the field that contains the length of the data being sent. The field name must be defined within the same record format, have a data type of S, be five digits in length with zero decimals, and have a usage of P.

```
....1....+....2....+....3....+....4....+....5....+....6....+....7....+....8
A          R FORMAT1               VARLEN(&LEN)
A            LEN           5S 0P
A            DATA          40A
```

Appendix

Double-Byte Character Sets

The term double-byte character set (DBCS) refers to those languages that require two bytes to define each character. Japanese and Chinese are two such languages.

The requirements for DBCS in DDS are just slightly different from standard single-byte character languages. This appendix discusses those differences for each file type. Also, special keywords are available when you are using DBCS. We provide here just a listing of these keywords without delving into the complete syntax of each.

DATA TYPES

With DBCS, you must use special codes to indicate that a field is a DBCS field. The following is a list of these codes and where they are allowed:

Code	Meaning	Where Used
J	Only — DBCS data	Physical, Logical, and Display Files
E	Either — DBCS or alphanumeric data allowed	Physical, Logical, and Display Files
O	Open — DBCS and alphanumeric data allowed	Physical, Logical, Display, Printer, and ICF Files
G	Graphic — DBCS data with no shift controls	Physical, Logical, Display, and Printer Files

KEYWORDS

No special keywords are available for physical, logical, and ICF files.

Display Files

The following keywords are used for DBCS fields only:

GRDATR (GRID ATTRIBUTE)

Used to define the default color and line type for a grid structure.

GRDBOX (GRID BOX)

Used to define the shape, positioning, and attributes for a box structure.

GRDCLR (GRID CLEAR)

Used to define a rectangle on a screen in which all current grid structures are clear from the screen.

GRDLIN (GRID LINE)
Used to define the shape, positioning, and attributes for a line structure.

GRDRCD (GRID RECORD)
Used to define a record format as a grid structure. Used in conjunction with GRDBOX and GRDLIN.

IGCALTTYP (ALTERNATIVE DATA TYPE)
Used to change an alphanumeric field to allow DBCS data.

IGCCNV (DBCS CONVERSION)
Used to permit use of DBCS conversion without your having to enter the DBCS characters directly from the keyboard.

Printer Files
DFNLIN (DEFINE LINE)
Used to draw a horizontal or vertical line.

IGCALTTYP (ALTERNATIVE DATA TYPE)
Used to change an alphanumeric field to a DBCS field.

IGCANKCNV (ALPHANUMERIC-TO-DBCS CONVERSION)
Used to change alphanumeric characters to the equivalent DBCS characters for the Japanese language only.

IGCCDEFNT (DBCS CODED FONT)
Used to specify the DBCS coded font for a field.

IGCCHRRTT (DBCS CHARACTER ROTATION)
Used to rotate DBCS characters 90 degrees on the printed page.

New Books in the 29th Street Press Library

THE AS/400 EXPERT: READY-TO-RUN RPG/400 TECHNIQUES

By Julian Monypenny and Roger Pence

As the first book in The AS/400 Expert series, *Ready-to-Run RPG/400 Techniques* provides a variety of RPG templates, subroutines, and copy modules, sprinkled with evangelical advice, to help you write robust and effective RPG/400 programs. Highlights include string-handling routines, numeric editing routines, date routines, error-handling modules, and tips for using OS/400 APIs with RPG/400. The tested and ready-to-run code building blocks — provided on an accompanying CD-ROM — easily snap into existing RPG code and integrate well with new RPG/400 projects. 203 pages.

DDS PROGRAMMING FOR DISPLAY & PRINTER FILES, SECOND EDITION

By James Coolbaugh

DDS Programming for Display & Printer Files, Second Edition helps you master DDS and — as a result — improve the quality of your display presentations and your printed jobs. Updated through OS/400 V4R3, the second edition offers a thorough, straightforward explanation of how to use DDS to program display files and printer files. It includes extensive DDS programming examples for CL and RPG that you can put to use immediately because a companion CD-ROM includes all the DDS, RPG, and CL source code presented in the book. 429 pages.

OPNQRYF BY EXAMPLE

By Mike Dawson and Mike Manto

The OPNQRYF (Open Query File) command is the single most dynamic and versatile command on the AS/400. Drawing from real-life, real-job experiences, the authors explain the basics and the intricacies of OPNQRYF with lots of examples to make you productive quickly. An appendix provides the UPDQRYF (Update Query File) command — a powerful addition to AS/400 and System /38 file update capabilities. 216 pages.

RAPID REVIEW STUDY GUIDES

Series Editor: Mike Pastore

You know that becoming a Microsoft Certified Systems Engineer can be lucrative. Still, seeking the certification isn't a goal for the faint of heart. Our Rapid Review Study Guides give you pre- and post-assessments to measure your progress, exam preparation tips, an overview of exam material, vocabulary drills, hands-on activities, and sample quiz questions on CD and in the book. Current titles include *Networking Essentials, Windows 95, System Management Server 1.2, Windows NT 4.0 Server, TCP/IP for Microsoft Windows NT 4.0, Windows NT 4.0 Workstation, Internet Information Server 4.0,* and *Windows NT 4.0 Server in the Enterprise.*

SQL/400 BY EXAMPLE

By James Coolbaugh

Designed to help you make the most of SQL/400, *SQL/400 by Example* includes everything from SQL syntax and rules to the specifics of embedding SQL within an RPG program. For novice SQL users, this book features plenty of introductory-level text and examples, including all the features and terminology of SQL/400. For experienced AS/400 programmers, *SQL/400 by Example* offers a number of specific examples that will help you increase your understanding of SQL concepts and improve your programming skills. 204 pages.

TCP/IP AND THE AS/400

By Michael Ryan

Transmission Control Protocol/Internet Protocol (TCP/IP) is fast becoming a major protocol in the AS/400 world because of TCP/IP's ubiquity and predominance in the networked world as well as its being the protocol for the Internet, intranets, and extranets. *TCP/IP and the AS/400* provides background for AS/400 professionals to understand the capabilities of TCP/IP, its strengths and weaknesses, and how to configure and administer the TCP/IP protocol stack on the AS/400. It shows TCP/IP gurus on other types of systems how to configure and manage the AS/400 TCP/IP capabilities. 362 pages.

ESSENTIALS OF SUBFILE PROGRAMMING
and Advanced Topics in RPG
By Phil Levinson

Essentials of Subfile Programming teaches you to design and program subfiles, offering step-by-step instructions and real-world programming exercises that build from chapter to chapter. You learn to design and create subfile records; load, clear, and display subfiles; and create pop-up windows. In addition, the advanced topics help you mine the rich store of data in the file-information and program-status data structures, handle errors, improve data integrity, and manage program-to-program communication. An instructor's manual is available. 260 pages.

IMPLEMENTING AS/400 SECURITY, THIRD EDITION
By Wayne Madden and Carol Woodbury

Concise and practical, this third edition of *Implementing AS/400 Security* not only brings together in one place the fundamental AS/400 security tools and experience-based recommendations that you need, but also includes specifics on the latest security enhancements available in OS/400 V4R1 and V4R2. In addition, you will find updated chapters that cover security system values; user profiles; database security; output queue and spooled file security; using OS/400 security APIs; network security; thwarting hackers; and auditing, as well as completely new chapters that include discussions about Internet security and business contingency planning. 424 pages.

INSIDE THE AS/400, SECOND EDITION
Featuring the AS/400e series
By Frank G. Soltis

Learn from the architect of the AS/400 about the new generation of AS/400e systems and servers, and about the latest system features and capabilities introduced in Version 4 of OS/400. Dr. Frank Soltis demystifies the system, shedding light on how it came to be, how it can do the things it does, and what its future may hold. 402 pages.

INTERNET SECURITY WITH WINDOWS NT
By Mark Joseph Edwards

Security expert and *Windows NT Magazine* news editor Mark Edwards provides the quintessential guide to Internet and intranet security from the Windows NT platform. This comprehensive book covers network security basics as well as IIS and MPS, and includes specific advice about selecting NT tools and security devices. The accompanying CD-ROM includes security-related utilities, tools, and software packages that, combined with the tips and techniques in the book, are powerful weapons in your security efforts. 520 pages.

MASTERING AS/400 PERFORMANCE
By Alan Arnold, Charly Jones, Jim Stewart, and Rick Turner

If you want more from your AS/400 — faster interactive response time, more batch jobs completed on time, and maximum use of your expensive resources — this book is for you. In *Mastering AS/400 Performance*, the experts tell you how to measure, evaluate, and tune your AS/400's performance. From the authors' experience in the field, they give you techniques for improving performance beyond simply buying additional hardware. 259 pages.

MASTERING THE AS/400, SECOND EDITION
A Practical, Hands-On Guide
By Jerry Fottral

With its utilitarian approach that stresses student participation, this introductory textbook to AS/400 concepts and facilities is a natural prerequisite to programming and database management courses. It emphasizes mastery of system/user interface, member-object-library relationship, use of CL commands, and basic database and program development utilities. The second edition is updated to V3R1/V3R6 and includes coverage of projection, selection, and access path with join logical files; the powerful new parameters added to the CHGPF command; and an introduction to SQL/400, with a focus on the Data Manipulation Language. Each lesson includes a lab that focuses on the essential topics presented in the lesson. 575 pages.

THE MICROSOFT OUTLOOK E-MAIL AND FAX GUIDE
By Sue Mosher

Sue Mosher explains the setup of individual e-mail services and components, e-mail options and when you might want to use them, and many time-saving techniques that take you beyond the basics. Users at all levels will learn from this comprehensive introduction to Microsoft's next generation of messaging software. The book includes coverage of the Internet Mail Enhancement Patch, Rules Wizard, and special features for Microsoft Exchange Server users. 500 pages.

PROGRAMMING IN RPG IV, REVISED EDITION

By Judy Yaeger, Ph.D., a NEWS/400 technical editor

This textbook provides a strong foundation in the essentials of business programming, featuring the newest version of the RPG language: RPG IV. Focusing on real-world problems and down-to-earth solutions using the latest techniques and features of RPG, this book provides everything you need to know to write a well-designed RPG IV program. This revised edition includes a new section about subprocedures and an addition about using the RPG ILE source debugger. An instructor's kit is available. 435 pages.

PROGRAMMING IN RPG/400, SECOND EDITION

By Judy Yaeger, Ph.D., a NEWS/400 technical editor

This second edition refines and extends the comprehensive instructional material contained in the original textbook and features a new section that introduces externally described printer files, a new chapter that highlights the fundamentals of RPG IV, and a new appendix that correlates the key concepts from each chapter with their RPG IV counterparts. Includes everything you need to learn how to write a well-designed RPG program, from the most basic to the more complex. An instructor's kit is available. 481 pages.

RPG IV JUMP START, SECOND EDITION
Moving Ahead With the New RPG

By Bryan Meyers, a NEWS/400 technical editor

In this second edition of *RPG IV Jump Start*, Bryan Meyers has added coverage for new releases of the RPG IV compiler (V3R2, V3R6, and V3R7) and amplified the coverage of RPG IV's participation in the integrated language environment (ILE). As in the first edition, he covers RPG IV's changed and new specifications and data types. He presents the new RPG from the perspective of a programmer who already knows the old RPG, pointing out the differences between the two and demonstrating how to take advantage of the new syntax and function. 214 pages.

VISUALAGE FOR RPG BY EXAMPLE

By Bryan Meyers and Jef Sutherland

VisualAge for RPG (VARPG) is a rich, full-featured development environment that provides all the tools necessary to build Windows applications for the AS/400. *VisualAge for RPG by Example* brings the RPG language to the GUI world and lets you use your existing knowledge to develop Windows applications. Using a tutorial approach, *VisualAge for RPG by Example* lets you learn as you go and create simple yet functional programs start to finish. The accompanying CD-ROM offers a scaled down version of VARPG and complete source code for the sample project. 236 pages.

WINDOWS NT MAGAZINE ADMINISTRATOR'S SURVIVAL GUIDE:
SYSTEM MANAGEMENT AND SECURITY

Edited by John Enck

In this first book in our Survival Guide™ series, John Enck has assembled the best articles and authors from *Windows NT Magazine* to share their experience with mission-critical system management and security issues. Topics include optimization, troubleshooting, boot failures, programming, installation, securing the Internet connection, testing, firewalls, data access, task managers, file servers, passwords, and more. 359 pages.

WINDOWS NT MAGAZINE ADMINISTRATOR'S SURVIVAL GUIDE:
NETWORKING AND BACKOFFICE

Edited by John Enck

In this second book in our Survival Guide™ series, John Enck has assembled the best *Windows NT Magazine* articles about networking and BackOffice issues. Topics include Remote Access Service; PPTP; assigning IP addresses and IP routing; name resolution with WINS, NetBIOS, and DNS; using NT with the Internet; telephony; NT Services for Macintosh; connectivity; performance tuning; clusters; enhancing SQL Server performance; implementing MS Exchange; Systems Management Server; and more. 469 pages.

FOR A COMPLETE CATALOG OR TO PLACE AN ORDER, CONTACT

29th Street Press
Duke Communications International
221 E. 29th Street • Loveland, CO 80538-2727
(800) 621-1544 • (970) 663-4700 • Fax: (970) 203-2756

OR SHOP OUR WEB SITE: **www.29thStreetPress.com**